GREEN
MARKETING

GREEN MARKETING

Jacquelyn A. Ottman

Foreword by Hubert H. "Skip" Humphrey III

NTC Business Books
a division of *NTC Publishing Group* • Lincolnwood, Illinois USA

Library of Congress Cataloging-in-Publication Data

Ottman, Jacquelyn A.
    Green marketing : challenges and opportunities for the new marketing age /
Jacquelyn Ottman.
        p.   cm.
    Includes index.
    1. Green marketing.   I. Title.
    HF5413.089   1992
    658.8′02—dc20   92-9423
                                                                                        CIP

 Printed on recycled
paper, using soy ink

1995 Printing

Published by NTC Business Books, a division of NTC Publishing Group.
4255 West Touhy Avenue, Lincolnwood (Chicago), Illinois 60646-1975, U.S.A.
© 1993 by J. Ottman Consulting, Inc. All rights reserved.
No part of this book may be reproduced, stored in a retrieval system,
or transmitted in any form or by any means,
electronic, mechanical, photocopying, recording or otherwise,
without the prior permission of NTC Publishing Group.
Manufactured in the United States of America.

    4 5 6 7 8 9 TS 9 8 7 6 5 4 3

Dedication

I wish to dedicate this book to all the people who are trying to improve the quality of the world around us, and to my parents who have done so much to enhance the quality of my life.

The Experts Praise This Timely Book

"*Green Marketing* shows that environmental business is good business. Jacquelyn Ottman identifies the important consumer trends that will transform U.S. corporations during the next several years. A great contribution!"

> William G. Rosenberg, Assistant Administrator for Air and Radiation
> United States Environmental Protection Agency

"Jacquelyn Ottman has written the definitive work on green marketing. Now's the time to decide what green will mean to your company—and to stay one step ahead of your competitors."

> Jeff Heilbrun, President
> American Marketing Association

"*Green Marketing* demonstrates that marketing is changing: It is becoming broader, more important, and potentially much more exciting. These changes offer marketing professionals tougher challenges *and* great opportunities."

> Dorothy Mackenzie, Director
> Dragon International

"Jacquelyn Ottman's book is a veritable Chinese menu of successful strategic and tactical options for green marketing, with a rich collection of supporting data. It is a powerful tool for helping companies to discover how turning green can help them earn serious money by tapping into this huge and growing purchasing preference of consumers."

> David Mager, Director of Environmental Standards
> Green Seal

"Consumers and product manufacturers alike have navigated their way through the new environmentalism that arose late in the last decade. Now, we have reached an era of ingrained environmental attitudes, characterized by our almost unconscious personal knowledge of what *we think* is or is not environmentally correct. Jacquelyn Ottman reveals that doing good for the environment along with enhancing the corporate bottom line truly can be a great marketing partnership."

Amy Barr, Director
Good Housekeeping Institute

Contents

FOREWORD

Fortune magazine tells us that environmentalism "may be the business issue of the decade"; already, 40 percent of all new household products feature an environmental claim in their labeling or advertising. This "green revolution" is not a fad or a flash in the pan. All else being equal, the product that is both environmentally superior and competitively priced will have an unbeatable edge in tomorrow's marketplace.

This is exciting news. In fact, I am convinced we are on the verge of what the management experts like to call a "paradigm shift"—a fundamental realignment of our mindset and expectations toward an enduring public ethic that expects every product to be designed to minimize its environmental impact. If you doubt me, ask your children. Ask them about teenage mutant turtles, "eco-warriors," and other super heroes who fight to save the planet from toxic wastes, ozone-depleting chemicals, and other environmental perils. For that matter, ask them about recycling, composting, or excessive packaging. They'll give you a glimpse of what's ahead.

The business that prospers in the future will be the business that anticipates these changes. That's where this book comes in. Jacquie Ottman understands, as well as any expert I know, that the "green revolution" is about more than simply *marketing* products as green. It's about ensuring that those products genuinely *are* green. Ensuring that the entire *company* is green. This process doesn't begin in the marketing department; it ends there. In this valuable and insightful primer, Jacquie Ottman guides her reader through every stage of that journey, from taking a good, long look at your company's culture, all the way to developing winning strategies for getting ahead of the curve and preempting the future.

Profound social changes are never painless, but in this case they can be immensely rewarding. As Tom Peters has said, the greening of the market is "a remarkable, perhaps once-in-a-century opportunity" for the corporation wise enough to seize it. The insights and advice that follow can give your company a head start toward capitalizing on that opportunity.

Hubert H. "Skip" Humphrey
Attorney General of Minnesota

PREFACE

Just a few years ago, superconcentrated laundry detergents gathered dust in a Denver test market. Paper towels made from recycled content were rejected as inferior, even unclean. And extra packaging added perceived value to competitive consumer products. More was more, whiter was better, and disposability was king. But all of this is rapidly changing. A new marketing age has arrived.

With garbage piling up in our communities, forests disappearing at an alarming rate, and the air getting harder to breathe, a revolution is underway to halt the misuse of our planet's resources. This revolution is taking place at our nation's supermarkets, drug stores, and mass merchandisers. To consumers concerned about the quality of their lives, less is now becoming more, and purchasing decisions are increasingly swayed by the impact that products have on the environment.

From now on, companies that don't respond to "green" issues with safer and more environmentally sound products risk falling out of sync with the consumer. And for marketers who *do* heed the consumer's call, opportunities abound. Sales at Church & Dwight, makers of Arm & Hammer baking soda, have grown from $16 million to $350 million due to a timely and thorough response to the trend. The concentrated refill for Procter & Gamble's Downy fabric softener cuts down on waste and is cheaper to produce than full strength alternatives. With a product that is kinder to the environment as well as to people, 3M has expanded the market for paint strippers.

This book is about the green marketing strategies for taking advantage of the myriad opportunities presented by environmental consumerism. It will introduce readers to the green revolution and help them understand its challenges. It will provide a glimpse into the future, with its abundance of growth opportunities.

Whether you are an entrepreneur, a marketing director, or a CEO, you will discover in this book how green marketing strategies can help you to develop products that cost less, work better, and last longer. You will learn how to communicate your environmental initiatives so as to enhance your company's and brands' images and build bridges to your consumers. Representing the gamut of products from household cleaning and laundry to food, fashion, appliances, and automobiles, case study examples will stimulate your thinking and provide you with models to follow. Perhaps most importantly, this book will help you understand how effective green marketing can be an agent of positive change within your company.

Take the time now to examine the environmental consumer trend while it is still in its infancy. A once-in-a-decade opportunity exists for marketers to green their products and processes and discover a potent source of competitive advantage, as well as personal reward.

ACKNOWLEDGMENTS

Like a true green marketing program, this book represents the combined input of many stakeholders in the realms of industry, government, and environmental groups. Several individuals, too many to mention, provided valuable information and case study examples. Some gave generously of their time to review the manuscript or provide other support. To them I extend my deepest appreciation: Mike Virgintino of 3M; Paul Ahern and Caroline Johnson of Ahern & Heussner; Robert Taber of Ally and Gargano; W. John Wright of the Angus Reid Group; Laura Klauberg of Chesebrough-Pond's; Bryan Thomlison of Church & Dwight; Deborah Cross of Coca-Cola; Robert Blanchard of Colgate-Palmolive; Michael Levy and Robert Hunt of Franklin Associates; Joseph Glick of Glick Associates; Glenda Goehrs of GSD&M; Martin Wolf, consultant to the Good Housekeeping Institute; David Mager and his colleagues at Green Seal; John Culligan of Lehn and Fink; Larry Power of McGrath/Power; Eric Goldstein, Esq., of the Natural Resources Defense Council; Frederick Elkind of Ogilvy & Mather; H.E. "Zeke" Swift of Procter & Gamble; Bray Fay of the Roper Organization; Cynthia Georgeson of S.C. Johnson and Son; Linda Brown of Scientific Certification Systems; Dr. Richard Kashmanian of the U.S. EPA; and Cynthia Drucker of Webster Industries, as well as colleagues and associates including Rosalind Chernoff, Catherine Dold, Patricia Grant,

Judith Grey, Allan Kaufman, Stella Kupferberg, Eric Miller, Richard Schwartz, Robert Stull, and Kathryn Wolfson.

I also wish to thank Eliot Tyler, Marjorie Vandenberg, and Jill Vohr who did a superb job of checking facts, editing, and researching case studies. Karen van Craenenbroeck rose to the occasion as administrative assistant extraordinaire. Finally, I wish to thank my editor, Anne Knudsen, of NTC Business Books, who shepherded the manuscript with grace and patience.

Jacquelyn A. Ottman
New York City
September 1992

Chapter 1

WHY TODAY'S MARKETERS MUST GO GREEN

In just a few short years, the environment has risen from a concern of the fringe to the top of the nation's agenda. People are concerned about protecting their lives and their livelihoods and are taking action at supermarket shelves, skewing purchases to products perceived as environmentally sound and rejecting those that are not. This is environmental consumerism and it is turning marketing upside down. While representing a potential threat for marketers who drag their feet, opportunities await those companies whose products and images are brought into line with consumers' growing environmental demands. Environmental consumerism represents profound implications for marketers; new strategies will be required to make the most of its opportunities. Time is of the essence. The environmental consumer trend is moving rapidly, and competitors around the world are already responding with substance. Those marketers who can tap into consumers' demands with

1

more environmentally sound products and establish their environmental credentials while attitudes are still forming stand to gain the most.

The Age of the Green Consumer

Environmental concerns rose to the surface in the 1970s, but subsided in response to a number of legislative initiatives designed to correct the problems. However, numerous environmental disasters and events in the late 1980s have pulled environmentalism into the spotlight once again. We've discovered the hole in the Earth's protective ozone layer. Medical waste is washing up on the shores of East Coast beaches. And

EXHIBIT 1.1
The Environment's Placement on the Public Agenda

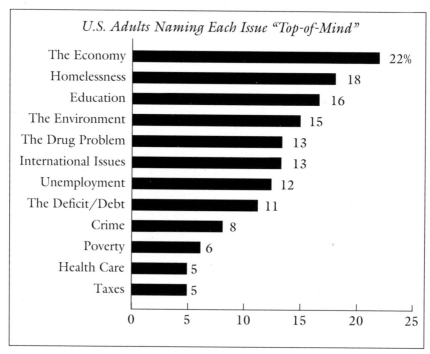

Source: *Environment U.S.A.*, The Angus Reid Group, 1991.

the media headlined the Mobro garbage barge's four month search for a dumpsite. Events like these have reignited the nation's interest and placed the environment squarely among the top public priorities. More than one in six adults surveyed in 1991 cited the environment as the most important issue facing the Unites States today. And while economic health is still the public's number one priority, more and more people are refusing to sacrifice environmental quality for the sake of a stronger economy.

Consumers' anxiety over environmental issues extends deep into mainstream America. An overwhelming majority now believe that pollution is a serious problem and is getting worse, continuing in the past 20 years to defile the very air we breathe and the water we drink (See Exhibits 1.2 and 1.3.).

EXHIBIT 1.2
U.S. Consumers' Concerns about Environmental Issues

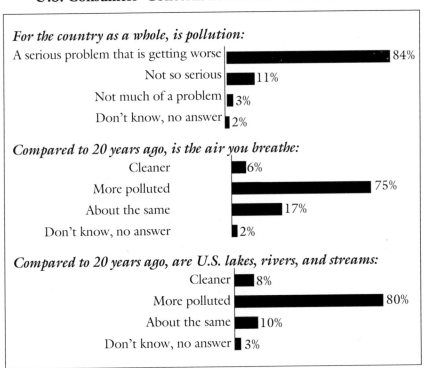

Source: *New York Times*/CBS News Poll, April 1990.

EXHIBIT 1.3
U.S. Consumers' Environmental Outlook

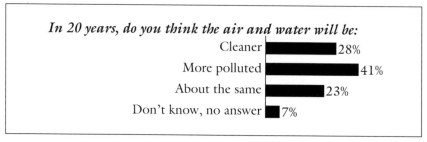

In 20 years, do you think the air and water will be:
- Cleaner — 28%
- More polluted — 41%
- About the same — 23%
- Don't know, no answer — 7%

Source: *New York Times*/CBS News Poll, April 1990.

Frequent industrial accidents such as the Three Mile Island nuclear episode, and the Exxon Valdez oil spill in Prince William Sound, Alaska, and reports of threats such as global climate change make our world seem out of control. Four out of ten Americans (41%) expect the state of their air and water will be worse 20 years from now.

It is one thing for people to perceive environmental ills as faraway phenomena, but it's another entirely when they are in our own backyards. Consumers are taking action on green issues because they have begun to hit home. Nightly news broadcasts show us environmental disasters on *our* beaches. We see *our* woodlands and wildlife destroyed. It's the garbage *we* generate that creates the need for new landfills in *our* neighborhoods. Almost daily we are faced with a litany of frightening statistics on cases of skin cancer, birth defects, chemical allergies, and a host of other illnesses that make us suspect our water is no longer fit to drink and that our food is not pure. Perceived as a direct threat to health and pocketbook, solid waste is fast becoming a top priority on the public worry list and is now on a par with air pollution. (See Exhibit 1.4.)

We in the United States are not alone. The decimation of Germany's Black Forest by acid rain, the accidental release of toxic chemicals into the Rhine River, the spread of a nuclear cloud from Chernobyl across Eastern Europe, and other disasters in the 1980s have rocketed awareness of environmental issues into the headlines and onto the political agendas of most other nations around the world.

A poll of 16 countries in 1992 found that more than four-fifths of respondents identified with the statement: "I am very worried about the

EXHIBIT 1.4
The Single Most Important Environmental Issue for Consumers

Issue	1989	1991
Air quality/pollution	30%	27%
Consumer solid waste/garbage disposal	12%	25%
Manufacturer/chemical/toxic waste	8%	5%
Other waste issues	10%	7%
Water quality/pollution	15%	13%
Ozone layer/greenhouse effect/fluorocarbons	14%	9%
Oil spills	3%	2%
Forest depletion	2%	4%
Other	3%	4%

Source: *Consumer Solid Waste, Awareness, Attitude, and Behavior Study III*, Gerstman & Meyers, 1991.

state of the environment." More than half concurred that "pollution must be reduced even if it means slower growth." (See Exhibit 1.5.) W. John Wright, senior vice president of research firm, The Angus Reid Group, sums it up: "Not one subject ultimately unites the earth in common concern but this one."[1]

Attempted fixes to environmental ills are being written into legislation at the federal, state, and local levels—a sure sign of the trend's grassroots permanence. In the past 20 years, we have witnessed a steady stream of federal statutes designed to purify our air and water, protect wildlife and endangered species, and clean up hazardous waste sites. These laws may pale in comparison to what is to come. Escalating anxiety about the quality of the environment has engendered support for stiff new laws aimed at making polluters pay. In fact, three-quarters of Americans believe the government should keep environmental protection a priority even if it means slower economic growth.[2] Legislation now being passed will place unprecedented demands on industry to minimize the envi-

EXHIBIT 1.5
Worldwide Environmental Concern

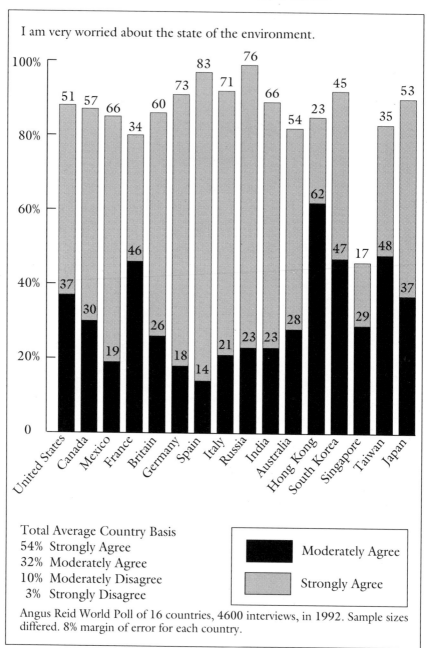

I am very worried about the state of the environment.

Total Average Country Basis
54% Strongly Agree
32% Moderately Agree
10% Moderately Disagree
 3% Strongly Disagree

■ Moderately Agree
▧ Strongly Agree

Angus Reid World Poll of 16 countries, 4600 interviews, in 1992. Sample sizes differed. 8% margin of error for each country.

Source: CNN/Angus Reid Group World Poll, 1992.

ronmental impact of manufacturing processes—a sign that green concerns are becoming a priority over business expediency.

Willingness to take action on environmental issues—both through legislative means and through changes in lifestyle—is at an all-time high. The *Yankelovich Monitor*, tracking concern for the environment since the early 1970s, reports that commitment to green issues reached an all-time high in 1990. And as shown in Exhibit 1.6, as of 1991 almost a quarter of adults are committed to *act on*, not just sympathize with, environmental concerns. No longer limited to society's radical fringe, those people willing to back up their belief in the clean environment with action cut across *all* demographic segments—the young, the old, the college educated, blue-collar workers, and so on.

EXHIBIT 1.6
Adult Population Strongly Committed to Protect/Improve the Environment

Year	*Percent*
1972	21%
1973	22
1974	20
1975	18
1976	19
1977	18
1978	18
1979	16
1980	19
1981	18
1982	17
1983	17
1984	15
1985	18
1986	16
1987	—
1988	—
1989	28
1990	29
1991	24

Source: *Yankelovich Monitor*, Yankelovich Clancy Shulman, 1991.

The most significant implication of this upturn for today's marketers of consumer products and services is that individuals are acting upon their values through *the power of their purchasing decisions*. Whereas in the past environmental sensitivity manifested itself primarily in corporate boycotts and in rallies aimed at the passage of environmental laws[3], in the 1990s consumers are voicing their concerns in the supermarket. They are shaping a new trend called *environmental consumerism*—an attempt by individuals to protect themselves and the planet by buying only products they consider "green" and leaving non-green products on the shelves.

In this new marketing age, products are being evaluated not only on performance or price, but on the social responsibility of manufacturers. Value now includes the environmental soundness of product and package. Increasingly, it will embrace the long-term impact of a product on society *after* it is used. Quality is an image that no longer stands apart from environmental impact.

People believe that the legislative initiatives enacted in the 1970s and 1980s failed to create long-term solutions. They see industry as playing a major role in environmental degradation and they are beginning to understand how social ills such as overpopulation can contribute to environmental ills. They are confident that industry possesses the technological prowess to clean up the mess but recognize the value of their own contributions. People are looking for simple, practical ways to get involved. And as consumers they are increasingly exercising the power of their purchasing decisions—their economic vote—to affect social and environmental change. Growing numbers of consumers are boycotting the products of companies with poor environmental and social records, while skewing their purchases to favor corporations they view as "socially responsible." As of 1992, 54% of Americans read labels to see if products were environmentally safe, 57% sought out products and packaging made from recycled materials, and 34% said they had boycotted a company that was careless towards the environment.[4] This creates strategic marketing opportunities for manufacturers who can demonstrate strong environmental performance. Marketers who do not will be penalized in the marketplace. Their products will lose value in the minds of consumers and their reputations will become tarnished.

Green: The New Value Added

The implications of environmental consumerism on an already intensely competitive marketplace are far-reaching. Overall market growth for many types of consumer products such as frozen entrees and cleaning aids has come to a virtual halt; value-priced alternatives are increasingly grabbing market share from major brands. Responsiveness to conventional advertising and marketing strategies is on the wane. More and more purchasing decisions are being made at the supermarket shelf.

The number of consumers who claim to be brand loyal has dropped from a high of 56% measured in 1988 to a record low of 46% in 1991.[5] Most consumers instead are purchasing among preferred *sets* of brands. While quality, price, and convenience are still uppermost in consumers' purchasing decisions, a fourth attribute—environmental compatibility (a product's greenness)—is fast becoming a tie-breaker at the shelf. *Packaging* magazine reports that as of 1991, 70% of consumers said that a product or package's recyclability has affected their purchasing decision. This reflects a 100% increase since 1986. The potential for "green" to sway purchasing decisions has not been lost on manufacturers of commodity-type products such as health and beauty aids, pet care, and household and laundry products. In these categories, green offerings represented 20 to 40% of all new products introduced in 1991.[6] With the environmental consumerism trend moving at its current speed, green attributes could soon be *de rigueur* for many categories of consumer products. In the 1990s, however, they still represent a potent source for competitive advantage.

Marketers of major brands have particular opportunities to bring their products and packaging into line with consumers' environmental expectations. Because consumers are familiar with them, environmentally enhanced versions of established brands may have an edge over new green brands from unknown manufacturers. That major brands have emerged as a popular target of environmentalists suggests that consumers want to continue to purchase them with the confidence of knowing it is environmentally acceptable to do so.

Opportunities Await

Increased market share is just one of the many potential benefits of corporate and product greening. Marketers are also discovering that developing environmentally sound products and manufacturing processes not only provides an opportunity to do the right thing, but it can also enhance corporate and brand image, save money, and open new markets for products catering to consumers' needs to maintain a high quality of life.

Intentionally or not, Americans are already adopting a wholesale environmental ethic. We bring back bottles, cans, and newspapers to be recycled and take steps to conserve energy at home. Our cars are powered by unleaded gasoline, and more and more households are daily consumers of energy-efficient appliances, low- or no-phosphate detergents, concentrated laundry products, and solar powered watches and calculators. Given recent buying trends, it is clear that consumers are eagerly going even further by adopting any number of preventive health practices and snapping up a whole host of new products that can improve their quality of life, as well as help them contribute to a better environment. Many of these products represent opportunities for *high margins* and *high volume*.

Read any trade publication to witness the stunning growth of products such as bottled water, new age all-natural soft drinks, air and water filtration devices, organic foods, and natural health and beauty aids. Discover how consumers' environmental concerns are creating new markets for alternative cleaning products such as baking soda, white vinegar, and lemon juice.

The sales of green household and personal care products are projected to increase fivefold to $9.6 billion by 1995.[7] With the nation's landfills closing at a rapid rate and drought conditions already the norm in the West, opportunities abound for products and packaging that help save natural resources and minimize waste.

Current buying trends may represent just the tip of the iceberg. Most green products are purchased now by an estimated 25% of shoppers who represent the most environmentally aware and committed of all consumers. They believe they can make an impact and know how to identify green products and where to get them. But a very large majority of consumers, while sympathizing with environmental concerns, has yet to respond in a substantive manner at the supermarket shelf. Just wait—awareness for environmental ills is growing along with an understanding for why and how consumers can get involved. Existing opportunities may pale in comparison to those that will become available when the buying power of these more passive green consumers is unleashed through further educational efforts coupled with easy, cost-effective solutions.

The Time to Proceed Is Now

The implications for marketers are clear. A swift and decisive response to consumers' environmental concerns is necessary to maintain market share and image. A special window of opportunity exists for marketers who act *now* while attitudes are still forming.

Many marketers, and especially those in the most environmentally sensitive and visible industries like chemicals, petroleum, or household cleaning products, have moved quickly. They have developed aggressive strategies and set up management systems to make sure their corporate environmental profiles and product offerings keep in step with or exceed consumer and regulatory demands. Many of these companies are now perfecting the technologies that will form the next generation of consumer products in which environmental impacts will be balanced with consumers' desires for performance, convenience, and affordable pricing.

Other marketers, however, have been slow to respond. Some are skeptical, claiming that environmental consumerism is no more than a passing fad, and are reluctant to begin what may be a costly series of changes in their operations and products. Many want to do the right thing but point to a lack of scientific and technical data that can help them define green for their products and processes. With the laws still being written, some of these companies are reluctant to get involved for fear of backlash from consumers, environmental groups, and the media.

But marketers can't afford to wait. The opportunities for environmental marketing outweigh the risks. All signs point to environmental consumerism as the marketing (if not the social, economic, *and* political) trend of the decade. Despite the confusion, the lack of rules, and the risk, the dynamics of environmental consumerism demand that every marketer begin to address the issues now.

The trend is moving faster than any other in recent history. By one researcher's 1990 estimate, there were 22 million green households in the United States (representing 23% of all households)—a number which will more than double to 52 million by 1995 and encompass 52% of all households.[8] (A green household includes consumers who intentionally buy green products as well as those consumers who buy green products on impulse.) Marketers who are proactive, who get out ahead of the curve while consumers are still forming their attitudes and shaping their environmental habits, will reap the biggest rewards.

Indeed, both domestic and international competitors are already vying for new marketing and sales opportunities. They are scrambling to overhaul their products and develop new ones. As of 1990, nearly seven in ten marketers (68%) had already begun to make environment-related changes in their packaging. This figure jumped from 59% in 1989.[9] A record number of products sporting green claims are fighting for space with ungreen products on supermarket shelves. In 1991 there were 810 green product introductions—representing 13.4% of total new products—up from a mere 24 in 1985. (See Exhibit 1.7.)

In international markets, our trading partners are green. In Germany, Switzerland, the Netherlands, and the United Kingdom solid waste has long been a critical issue. Germany, the Netherlands, Italy, and France have had solid waste reduction and trash separation programs for more than five years.[10] Our trading partners' environmental purchasing sentiment is deeper than ours. Research conducted by the Backer Spielvogel Bates advertising agency found that while 67% of U.S. consumers said they would switch brands to choose one that comes in an environmentally safe package, a larger proportion of consumers in other countries would do so: 90% in the former East Germany, 88% in the former West Germany, 84% in Italy, and 82% in Spain.[11] A wide range of green products, including food, beverages, household cleaners, and health and beauty aids is rapidly being launched in many foreign countries. (See Exhibit 1.8.)

While products and packaging will need to be brought into line with escalating consumer and regulatory demands, companies need to be

EXHIBIT 1.7
Share and Number of New Green Product Introductions:
1985–1991

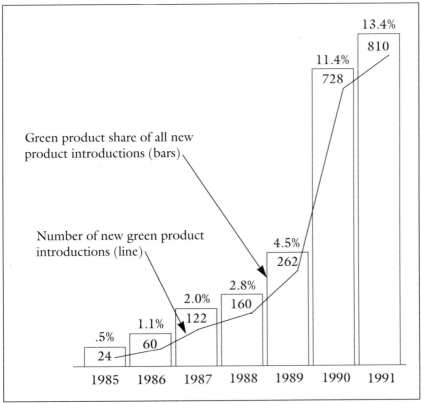

Source: New Green Products, 1985–91. Marketing Intelligence Service Ltd., 1991.

seen as environmentally responsible. In the age of environmental consumerism, the perception is the reality. Via aggressive media campaigns, competitors are communicating their environmental credentials to a broad base of constituents comprised of consumers, environmental groups, legislators, and retailers. Their objectives: to firmly establish a reputation in the environmental forefront. According to the J. Walter Thompson advertising agency the number of environment-themed print and television advertisements more than quadrupled between 1989 and 1990, from 41 to 212. (See Exhibit 1.9.)

Foot draggers beware. With green products and technologies in hand, international competitors are poised to steal precious market

EXHIBIT 1.8

Importance of Green Products by Country

	1986	1987	1988	1989	1990	1991
	total packaged goods introductions making green promises					
Canada	2.0%	0.6%	1.1%	4.6%	16.4%	33.9%
Australia	0.3	—	2.9	3.1	12.3	5.1
Europe*	0.7	0.9	0.7	2.4	5.7	3.2
Japan	0.2	0.7	1.6	1.8	1.5	0.8
South Africa	0.5	—	1.1	4.4	6.1	6.1
United Kingdom	0.9	2.4	4.0	8.3	10.8	7.2
United States	1.1	2.0	2.8	4.5	11.4	13.4

*Denmark, France, Germany, Italy

Source: Marketing Intelligence Service Ltd., Naples, NY, 1992.

share from U.S. companies. Their technological prowess promises more products and still greater competition. This could spell disaster for U.S. companies who fail to respond to consumers' environmental needs with haste.

As Richard Kashmanian, Ph.D., a senior economist at the U. S. Environmental Protection Agency (EPA) reminds us, "Environmentalism stretches beyond United States boundaries. If we don't sell more environmentally sound products in this country, other countries will. We will lose out on opportunities to sell these products to U.S. consumers and consumers abroad."

In stark contrast to the United States where industries such as automotive and energy have been slow to craft technological solutions to

EXHIBIT 1.9

Growth in Green Ads: 1989–1990

Media	1989	1990	*Change*
Print	32	170	+430%
TV	9	42	+367%

Source: J. Walter Thompson Company, *Greenwatch, No. 3.*, Spring/Summer 1991.

long-term environmental problems, international competitors recognize the potential for turning environmental issues into opportunities. In *Global Environmental Politics*, Janet Brown and Gareth Porter observe that European businesses view the control of greenhouse gases "not as a threat but as an opportunity for upgrading their technological bases and becoming more competitive in the world economy."[12] A survey of European executives found that 70% of European industries had plans to improve their environmental performance.[13] Already, products marketed by European-based firms are appearing on U.S. supermarket shelves—the Ecover line of all-natural laundry detergent and cleaning products, Melitta natural brown coffee filters, and The Body Shop line of toiletries and cosmetics represent just a few.

Japan is poised to emerge as a leader in environmental technology in the 21st century. Despite a poor record on wildlife preservation among other environmental issues, the Japanese have created impressive pollution prevention and energy conservation technologies. Keidanren, Japan's main business organization, has adopted an environmental charter that encourages Japanese companies to create environmental departments. The Ministry of International Trade's New Earth 21 blueprint attempts to reduce carbon dioxide emissions by the end of the 21st century, and an organization named Research Institute for Innovative Technology for Earth is in development. Japan and Germany are producing stunning advances in electric automobiles and solar batteries, among other achievements. Japan's Honda Motor Corporation has already unveiled its 1992 Civic VX, which seats five people and gets 50 miles per gallon—a feat that U.S. automakers have claimed was unachievable without a major downsizing of vehicles.[14]

Eco-labels, sponsored by governmental or quasi-governmental agencies, are proliferating in our trading partner countries. Created in 1977, Germany's Blue Angel logo appears on over 3,100 products in 57 categories to help consumers identify environmentally preferable products (See Exhibit 1.10.). Canada has issued Environmental Choice, guidelines for products ranging from paints to reusable cloth diapers. Japan has its own Ecomark program. Several other countries including Austria, Denmark, France, Holland, and New Zealand as well as the EC are also developing eco-labels of their own. While serving a need for environmentally conscious consumers in their own countries, these eco-labeling programs could be viewed as a form of protectionism with the

EXHIBIT 1.10
Germany's Blue Angel Seal

potential to lock out U.S. consumer goods unless our technologies and programs can keep pace.

Personal Rewards, Too

While the economic rewards of going green are abundant, there are many professional and personal rewards, too. This is one reason why environmental response is becoming second nature to progressive corporations. As more and more marketers are discovering each day, developing more environmentally correct processes and products offers a rare opportunity to integrate our own values into the workplace, to exercise our personal desire to make a contribution to environmental cleanup, and to help ensure a more secure future for our children.

In contrast to perceived consumer needs, like whether our clothes are "whiter than white," and our breath is "fresher than fresh," environmental issues are *real*, some are even life-threatening. Marketers who get involved now have a chance to make a big impact as individuals, for they will become part of a very select few who have the power to develop and market not just any new products, but products capable of empowering million of individuals to make the world a better place.

Environmental consumerism is a complex social trend as well as marketing phenomenon. Green consumers shop with a different agenda from their 1970s and 1980s predecessors. Thus, effectively addressing their needs requires new strategies. In the next chapter, we define who these new green consumers are and detail their buying strategies and behavior. In succeeding chapters we will outline the many challenges for green marketing and detail strategies for taking advantage of its opportunities. We will conclude with a glimpse into the future.

Notes

1. Telephone conversation with W. John Wright, senior vice president, The Angus Reid Group, Apr. 24, 1992.

2. *Environment U.S.A.*, The Angus Reid Group, Toronto, Canada, 1991.

3. The National Environment Protection Act, the Clean Air Act, the Clean Water Act, the Toxic Substances Control Act, the Resource Conservation and Recovery Act, and the Comprehensive Environmental Response Conservation and Liability Act (Superfund), among others were enacted in those two decades.

4. *Environmental Behavior, North America: Canada, Mexico, United States*, The Roper Organization, July 1992, commissioned by S.C. Johnson & Son.

5. *The Public Pulse*, The Roper Organization, October, 1991, p.6.

6. Marketing Intelligence Service, Ltd., Naples, NY, 1991.

7. *The Green Consumer*, FIND/SVP, 1990, p.16.

8. *Ibid*. p.6.

9. "A Study of the Attitudes of Industry Toward Using Environment-Friendly Packaging," conducted by Gallup for Walter Dorwin Teague Associates, Inc., 1990.

10. A.D. Little, Co. "Perspectives: The Green Consumer," pamphlet, 1990.

11. Alvin A. Achenbaum, "A Global View of Consumer Environmental Trends and the Advertising Community's Response," presented at the American Marketing Association's "Environmental Conference: Green Marketing from a Marketer's Perspective," Oct. 1991.

12. "Behind the Green Facade," Marnie Stetson, *Worldwatch* M/A, 1992, p.38.

13. *Ibid*.

14. *Ibid*., p.39.

Chapter 2

ENVIRONMENTAL CONSUMERISM: ENDURING TREND, MAJOR OPPORTUNITY

Environmental consumerism is being propelled by maturing Baby Boomers motivated by a desire to protect the quality of their lives and preserve the environment for their children. Bringing their environmental and social values with them into maturity, Baby Boomers are ushering in a permanent shift in values toward more environmentally sound products and companies. Educated, influential and upscale, green consumers wield enormous buying power, but addressing their needs poses many challenges: they are not willing to give up product attributes such as performance, quality, and convenience in their quest for green. However, marketers who can meet their needs have a golden opportunity to secure the loyalty of the most committed greens, as well as the host of passive green consumers they influence.

Baby Boomers in the Lead

Trends catch on fast when they are nurtured by a strong demographic force. The environmental consumerism trend is driven by the largest demographic group our nation has ever had—the maturing Baby Boom population.

By dint of sheer numbers, the 77 million Baby Boomers born between 1946 and 1964 have had a profound impact on society at every stage of their development. Their tastes in music, food, and fashion largely shape pop culture. Their most indelible mark on society is now emerging in the form of environmental consumerism.

In the 1990s, the Boomers will represent more than one-third of the U.S. population. By mid-decade, they will all be over the age of 30, with some well into their 40s. They have settled down, are raising children, and are assuming positions of power within society. Their decisions are shaped by deep-rooted values.

Recall that the Boomers were the first health- and fitness-conscious generation. That consciousness is now being merged with their reignited environmental concerns into a more holistic wellness philosophy that emphasizes overall quality of life.

The Boomers were the original activists—anti-war, anti-big business, and pro-environment. It was the Boomers who created the first Earth Day back in 1970. The Clean Air Act of 1970 and Clean Water Act of 1972, among other initiatives, sprang from their concern and activism.

The Boomers are not only numerous, they are sophisticated and smart. The most educated generation yet (27% of all 35–44-year-olds are college educated), they have access to more information than any other generation in history and they know how to use it. They consider themselves logical and rational, and are attracted to high quality and substance; they shun glitter and glitz. As they approach middle age and their highest income-producing years, they have the wherewithal to expect, demand, and pay for quality.

New Purchasing Ethic Emerging

Environmental consumerism is not another fad like oat bran or hoola hoops. Rather it is a long-term trend reflecting a permanent shift in societal values. For the Boomers, the move into middle age triggers a natural shift in focus—from acquisition in the household-forming years to quality of life and fulfillment. Quality of life is measured by the condition of one's home, community, and the world at large, and by family and personal health and well-being.

Spurred on by guilt over their contribution to environmental ills, the Boomers are merging their purchasing orientation with their environmental concerns and social values. Less is suddenly becoming more as Boomers demonstrate their environmental concerns by buying smaller, concentrated products that use less packaging, less glitzy products made by smaller (sounding) companies, less risky products that are made with fewer toxins and, in general, present less to worry about.

Many consumers are already adopting new values that can be summarized as a shift from quantity to quality, from short term to long term, and from me to we. Greed is being pushed aside for green, disposability and consumption are no longer appreciated for their own sakes. (See Exhibit 2.1.)

EXHIBIT 2.1
Hallmarks of the Age of Environmental Consumerism

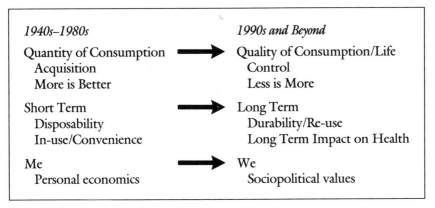

1940s–1980s	*1990s and Beyond*
Quantity of Consumption ⟶	Quality of Consumption/Life
Acquisition	Control
More is Better	Less is More
Short Term ⟶	Long Term
Disposability	Durability/Re-use
In-use/Convenience	Long Term Impact on Health
Me ⟶	We
Personal economics	Sociopolitical values

Source: J. Ottman Consulting, Inc., 1992.

FROM QUANTITY TO QUALITY

With their basic needs satisfied and surrounded by a plethora of now meaningless gadgets like gelato machines and espresso makers acquired during a 1980s shopping spree, consumers are no longer involved with "How many things can I *have?*" Attempting to gain control over their consumption, they are now asking, "How many things do I *need?*" They are concluding that less is more; enough is enough.

Environmental issues are quality of life issues and as such are part of an overall societal trend toward health maintenance. Reflecting a long-term decline, the nation's alcohol consumption rate is now near 1970s lows and anti-smoking is the norm. AIDS, the recession of the early 1990s, and a backlash against the greedy 1980s have dictated that conspicuous consumption is out, "moderation, seriousness, and social responsibility are in."[1]

Consumers appear to be no longer preoccupied with materialism and newness. Polls have long shown that materialism does not equate with happiness. Consumers with all the latest gadgets feel no better off than consumers of 30 years ago. Researchers for the *Yankelovich Monitor* have even found a five-year trend that shows new products are losing appeal with consumers. They attribute this to two factors: a growing dislike for shopping in general and the perception that new is risky.[2] After all, things take time to care for. But busy consumers, and especially sandwiched Baby Boomers, want time to enjoy life. Their watchwords are streamline and simplify—quality, not quantity.

When it comes right down to it, the term "green consumer" is an oxymoron. Consuming uses up valuable natural resources and creates waste. Individuals cannot live for long with this inconsistency. Expect them to increasingly ask: "Is this product really necessary?"

FROM SHORT TERM TO LONG TERM

Thanks to the Baby Boom and the growing affluence of their parents in the expanding post-War economy, the population of the United States as of 1990 is more than double that of 1940, there are five times as many cars on the roads, and the amount of garbage has piled up accordingly. In the past few decades disposability has become synonymous with affluence itself. However, the environmental implications of decades of free-wheeling consumption and trash disposal are now apparent. Consumers perceive convenience products such as disposable diapers and fast food packaging as major contributors to garbage pile-ups.

Consumer are increasingly adjusting their view of products in relation to time. In our fast-paced society, the convenience benefits of disposability are irresistible. While these attributes will not be tossed aside soon, they are progressively being re-evaluated with a growing appreciation for a product's long-term fate in the environment. Prompted by growing awareness of the implications of their consumption, consumers are starting to ask in an unprecedented fashion, "What happens to this product after I use it?"

Similarly, consumers are increasingly drawing a connection between environmental ills and their impact on long-term health. Just as they associate heart disease with a steady diet of consuming fatty foods, so too consumers perceive a long-term impact on their health of chemicals present in their food and in their homes. For example, a majority of consumers now believes that chemicals and preservatives used in the production and processing of food can impair health either directly, by eating food products containing these chemicals, or indirectly, by leaving a harmful residue in the earth's soil and groundwater supply.[3] Also, 69% of all consumers surveyed in a recent poll are concerned that the environmental situation today is already triggering an upturn in health problems. Alarmed by reports of lasting chemical build-ups in body tissue, consumers want to know: "If I use this aerosol oven cleaner for 20 years, will I get cancer?" and "Just how safe can the pesticides on my kids' apples be?"

The more educated and enlightened consumers are taking action—they are beginning to shun risky products and the companies who make them. This is reflected in the rapidly rising sales at natural foods stores. Marian Burros writes that natural food supermarkets are best defined by "what they don't have than what they do . . . no refined sugars; no refined white flours; no synthetic sweetners; no caffeine; no alcohol; no hydrogenated oil, tropical oils or cottonseed oils; no growth-promoting drugs; no bleaching; no preservatives, artificial colors, or flavors; no irradiation; no animal testing." In 1990, overall sales of natural foods were $4.22 billion, up 7.4% over 1989.[4]

Consumers pay, on average, 20% more for food in natural food super-markets, but the extra cost seems worth it, at least to one shopper who claims, "I don't care. I'll pay triple the price. I don't pay the doctor."[5]

FROM ME TO WE

In the 1980s the individual was king. Achievements and personal excellence were held in high esteem. Individualism was reflected in consumer choices and products proliferated to better serve the needs of a highly fragmented marketplace. In the 1990s a social conscience now reigns, with the emphasis moving away from the individual and placed instead on "how we relate to each other and act together to deal with global problems against which the individual seems powerless."[6] Whereas in the 1980s we purchased products with an eye toward meeting immediate needs, today we are increasingly paying attention to a product's broader implications.

One manifestation of this is that a growing number of consumers are making brand decisions based on manufacturers' records of achievement on environmental and social criteria—their compliance with environmental regulations, their hiring practices, and their trading policies with developing countries. An outgrowth of response to the South African boycotts of the 1970s, this trend toward corporate social responsibility acknowledges the potential for corporations to help create a more equitable world and to allow greater access to its resources by all citizens, including future generations who will feel the impact of corporate activity in the decades to come.

The corporate social responsibility trend even has its own consumer guidebook: *Shopping for a Better World*. It is published by the Council on Economic Priorities (CEP), a 22-year-old non-profit research group located in New York City. Now in its third edition and in the hands of nearly a million upscale and educated/influential consumers, this guidebook shows consumers how they can help the environment and contribute to solving various societal problems by skewing purchases toward companies with outstanding rewards for environmental and social achievement. The pocket guide lists over 2,400 popular brands of consumer products according to their manufacturers' records on 11 social criteria such as minority hiring practices, corporate giving, and animal testing.

According to CEP's research, 78% of readers have changed brands after reading the guide. While sales of specific brands may not be affected in the short term, the influential nature of the book's readers and the growing popularity of corporate social responsibility could eventually be significant. Over time, for example, association with a low-ranked corporation such as RJR Nabisco could prove detrimental to even such a well-loved brand like Oreo Cookies (made by Nabisco), while brands linked to highly rated corporations—particularly brands which share the corporate name, such as Colgate-Palmolive's Colgate Toothpaste—could benefit significantly.

S.C. Johnson has recognized that corporate image will become increasingly important in individual brand sales. Jane Hutterly, vice president environmental affairs, reports that her company has launched a multi-faceted program to communicate a positive corporate image. Along with several other initiatives, the company co-promotes its family of products including Glade and Pledge in conjunction with environmental groups. They work closely with the CEP to provide information for *Shopping for A Better World*, which Hutterly believes gets into the hands of influentials who have a disproportionate effect on consumers. The company also has adopted a corporate theme—"People Working for a Better World"—which is now emblazoned on corporate communiques.

At Procter & Gamble, CEO Edwin Artzt acknowledges that "Consumer attitudes towards our brands are increasingly affected by the image and reputation of the Procter & Gamble company. . . . The integrity of the company and its policies and practices in areas affecting the environment, nutrition, the safety of our raw materials, the social consciousness of our people and policies—all of these things today can have a bearing on the way the consumer feels about our brands." Writing in *Moonbeams*, P&G's inhouse magazine, Artzt urges employees to market the company with the same care and skill that they bring to all P&G brands. Acknowledging a change in strategy, he continues, "It is still our policy that our brands must stand on their feet, but the Company today must visibly stand behind them."

The desire for a better world touches all aspects of life. A growing number of people are volunteering, attending religious services, and donating money to charities. These trends, coupled with value shifts in consumer purchasing, suggest that the environmental consumerism movement is about much more than saving trees; it's about a move toward a more *humane* society that is attempting to replace materialistic consumption with a balance between economic growth at the expense of the environment and a simpler way of life. An evolution is underway that favors more intangible product benefits. In the words of Richard Adams, director of the New Consumer Institute (the UK counterpart of the CEP), this is forcing ". . . a sea change in corporate business and marketing practices, characterized by an agenda of integrity and complete corporate commitment." He adds, "The 'I shop, therefore I am' attitude is changing. The distinctive paradox of purchasing capacity equalling social value is being tackled in the name of global concern and basic human decency."[7]

Willis Harman, president of the Institute of Noetic Sciences and author of *Global Mind Change* and *Creative Work*, explains the shift as a movement from a society in which economics is dominant to one in which values and purpose are more important. He sees a "coming together of three outlooks on the world: the Western tradition with its emphasis on learning to manipulate the outer world; Eastern thought which concentrates on inner experience; and a third (influence) from indigenous peoples who emphasize a connectedness with nature."[8] He predicts that we will see the decomposition of some big institutions: banking systems, insurance systems, health care systems, and even large transnational corporations. He sees us moving toward smaller institutions or smaller, more autonomous parts of big ones. He sees big businesses changing and becoming less hierarchical. States Harman, "Businesses are hearing the voices of the people who want different control structures, who want more sense of purpose. They want the corporation to do meaningful things and they want it to be environmentally responsible."[9]

The environmental consumer trend will only accelerate and eventually become a permanent part of our culture. The leading edge of the Baby Boom is in its mid 40s. As the rest of the Boomers move into middle age and beyond, their demands for a high quality of life expressed as maintenance of personal health and well-being will only intensify. As they climb up the corporate ladders and assume full leadership in their communities, they will increasingly make their values felt, adding inter-

nal and external pressures for corporate and product greening and overall ethical performance.

The Green Consumer Is Your Best Customer

Environmentally conscious consumers can be defined as those who ac-
tively seek out products perceived as having relatively minimal impact
on the environment. Educated, affluent, and mainstream, they represent the most desirable of consumer targets. A potentially more lucrative, much larger target is the mass of passive green consumers who can
be motivated by cost-effective, easy-to-execute environmental solutions.

Polls and empirical data suggest that the typical green consumer is a
woman who is educated, affluent, and politically liberal. She is likely to
be between the ages of 30-49, has children six years old and older, and
resides in a Northeast, West, or Midwest suburb. Having adopted an
environmental consciousness in her youth, she is motivated by a desire
to protect her health and that of her children and to preserve the planet
for future generations. She is also likely to be influential in the community, and is possibly an activist, rallying support among her peers for local, environmental, or social causes. Her buying power—and her potential to influence her peers—makes this green consumer one of the most
desirable targets for marketers. (See Exhibit 2.2.)

That women are in the forefront of green cannot be underestimated—
they are primary shoppers and influence the purchasing decisions of the rest
of society and the next generation. A 1990 poll by the Warwick, Baker &
Fiore advertising agency found that across a broad range of categories,
women placed significantly higher importance on environmental purchasing criteria than men. The agency hypothesizes, "Women feel more vul-
nerable to the world around them while men have more of an inner sense of
control. Thus, men may feel more able to take control in general and,
therefore, feel somewhat less threatened by environmental issues."[10]

EXHIBIT 2.2
Demographic Profile of Most Environmentally
Active U.S. Consumers

	Total Public	Most Environmentally Active Consumers*
Sex		
Male	47%	40%
Female	53	60
Median Age	41	42
Median income (\$ in thousands)	28	34
Education		
Less than HS	19	10
HS graduate	38	30
Some college	24	32
Coll. grad. or more	18	27
Occupation		
Executive/prof.	16	23
White collar	18	19
Blue collar	26	20
Employed part-time	13	14
Employed full-time	48	49
Marital status		
Married	57	66
Single	43	34
Children under 13	34	39
Region		
Northeast	21	25
Midwest	25	27
South	33	25
West	20	23

*Profile of True-Blue Greens.

Source: *Environmental Behavior, North America: Canada, Mexico, United States*, The Roper Organization, commissioned by S. C. Johnson & Son, 1992.

Of course not all green consumers are as committed or as active as the people described here—there are many shades of green.

A Profile of the Green Consumer

Joseph Winski may have drawn the most accurate possible thumbnail character sketch of the green consumer, in an article in *Advertising Age,* derived from DDB Needham Worldwide's Life Style Study.

> I'm a 46-year-old mother. I am a homemaker, and I take my role as the "family caretaker" seriously, but I have a professional career outside the home, too. I certainly don't hold the "traditional" view of women in society.
>
> I'm keenly interested in news and politics. I try to be active in the community.
>
> I'm not reluctant to express my opinion, sometimes by writing letters to newspapers.
>
> I like to cook and bake and think it's important to do so. I am nutrition-conscious and avoid foods high in salt, sugar, or fat. I feel guilty about serving my family convenience foods.
>
> I make a detailed shopping list. I check ingredients and prices carefully.
>
> I like to discuss products with friends. I consult *Consumer Reports* and other published information for comparative product information.
>
> In advertising, I look for useful information. I don't like sex in advertising. I believe a lot of advertising, especially that on TV, is condescending to women. Insult me and I won't buy your product.
>
> I believe commercials for beer and wine and commercials aimed at children should be taken off TV. I also think there's too much sex and violence on TV.
>
> I think pollution is a serious threat to our health. Even if it means reducing our standard of living, we should toughen our pollution standards.
>
> I believe the individual can make a difference in cleaning up the environment. To me, environmentalism isn't a fad that will go away. Portray it as a hip or trendy thing and you'll turn me off.[11]

The Many Shades of Green

Commitment to environmental concerns within the population can be segmented by lifestyles, suggesting a diversity of green that has yet to be tapped. The most environmentally committed consumers represent a core of nearly 25% of upscale, educated individuals who say they are willing to pay a premium or forego certain conveniences to ensure a cleaner environment. On the other end of the spectrum, about 35% of the public are doggedly non-environmentalists, characterized more by indifference than anti-environmentalist leanings; they are downscale. The remainder of the public is more or less pro-environmental—they label themselves "environmentalist" when pollsters ask, but for various reasons described later are not fully acting on their concerns.

In 1992, the Roper Organization identified five segments within the U.S. population, each with a different level of environmental commitment, described as follows.

True-Blue Greens	20%	Active environmentalists
Greenback Greens	5%	
Sprouts	31%	The swing group
Grousers	9%	Not active environmentalists
Basic Browns	35%	

TRUE-BLUE GREENS

These 37 million people hold strong pro-environmental beliefs and live them. They are almost three times more likely than other consumers to avoid buying products from a company with a questionable environmental reputation, and twice as likely to buy greener types of products. They are the oldest of the groups (median age 42 years), the wealthiest, and the most likely to be married with children under 13. They tend to live in the East, the West, and the Midwest. Six in ten of them are women. They believe they can personally make a difference in solving environmental problems. A demographic profile of them is reflected in Exhibit 2.2.

GREENBACK GREENS

These 9 million people support environmentalism, more by giving money than by giving time or action. They are the most willing to spend

EXHIBIT 2.3
Activities that Different Segments Participate in Regularly to Protect the Environment

	U.S. Public	True-Blues	Green-backs	Sprouts	Grousers	Basic Browns
At purchase:						
Read labels	24%	62%	37%	22%	13%	3%
Use biodegradable plastic garbage bags	28	55	28	31	25	8
Avoid buying aerosols	28	61	42	35	16	4
Avoid products from specific companies	12	30	24	9	12	2
Buy products made from/ packed in recycled material	19	70	27	7	10	1
Buy products in refillable packaging	18	46	35	12	13	4
Avoid restaurants using styrofoam containers	8	21	12	6	5	2
After purchase:						
Return bottles, cans	58	86	69	76	46	25
Recycle newspapers	43	80	53	60	24	9
Sort trash	35	68	51	45	27	7
Other:						
Contribute money to environmental groups	8	20	19	5	7	1
Cut down on car use	8	20	13	5	11	2
Write to politicians	4	12	10	4	4	—

Source: *Environmental Behavior, North America: Canada, Mexico, United States*, The Roper Organization, commissioned by S. C. Johnson & Son, Inc., 1992.

considerably more for green products—a 15% price increase is acceptable to them for a representative sample of eight kinds of products. A little more than half (52%) are men. They are the youngest (median age 35), and the best educated (63% have some college) of all the groups. They are also more likely to be employed full time and to live on the West Coast. They feel too busy to change their lifestyles but they are happy and able to express their beliefs with their pocketbooks and wallets.

SPROUTS

Almost one-third of the U.S. public falls into this group. Sprouts want more pro-environmental legislation but don't believe that they themselves can do much to make a positive environmental impact. They regularly engage in pro-environmental activity but are not willing to pay more for pro-environmental products. They become uncertain when forced to choose between the environment and the economy. They are relatively affluent and well-educated and in other respects reflect a balance of middle America, with sex, age, and urban/rural splits close to the national norms. This is the swing group that can go either way on any environmental issue.

GROUSERS

This group of 17 million people takes few environmental actions but believes that other consumers aren't doing their part either, that business should be fixing the problems, and that green products cost too much more than their non-green counterparts and don't work well. They have slightly below-average educations and incomes; they feel confused and uninformed about environmental issues. They think the whole thing is someone else's problem and that someone else should fix it.

BASIC BROWNS

This largest group of more than 64 million people (35% of the public) is by far the least involved in environmentalism. They are half as likely as the average American to recycle bottles or cans (25% versus the 58% average); and only a fraction read product labels for their environmental information (3% versus the 24% average). This group is disproportionately male, Southern, blue-collar, and economically downscale. Their basic belief is that there is just not much that individuals can do to make a difference.

As noted in Exhibit 2.3, environmental behavior varies significantly across these segments, suggesting that not all categories of products or individual brands are affected equally by consumers' environmental concerns. A close look at the behavior of the most active segment, the True Blues, demonstrates the relative depth of their commitment. Given their societal influence, this suggests the types of behavior that can be expected from a much bigger group of consumers in the future. More than half of the True Blues return bottles and cans, read labels, recycle newspapers, and use "biodegradable" products on a regular basis. As social and style leaders, their forceful presence can be expected to exert increasing peer pressure, particularly on the Greenback Greens and the Sprouts—underscoring the opportunities of marketers who can win the loyalty of these influential True-Blues now.

Green Consumer Psychology and Buying Strategies

While consumers express their environmental concerns in individual ways, all green consumers appear to be motivated by universal needs. (See Exhibit 2.4.) These needs translate into new purchasing strategies with profound implications for the way products are developed and marketed.

NEED FOR INFORMATION

Individuals contribute to environmental clean-up and preservation primarily through product-related behavior such as recycling and purchasing products that are perceived as environmentally sound. In making their decisions, they want information about how to identify green

EXHIBIT 2.4
Green Consumer Psychology and Buying Strategies

Needs		Strategies
Information	➡	Read labels
Control	➡	Take preventive measures
Make a difference/ alleviate guilt	➡	Switch brands
Maintain lifestyles	➡	Buy interchangeable alternatives

Source: J. Ottman Consulting, Inc., 1992.

products and where to get them. In 1992, Roper found that 54% of consumers read labels at least occasionally. This figure rises to a whopping 95% for the True-Blue Greens. Research conducted by Procter & Gamble shows that consumers want even more information than currently available on product labels and in advertising.[12] They appear willing to go great lengths to get it: all of the major household-product companies have noted significant increases of environment-related calls to their consumer hotlines in the past few years.

Not surprisingly, the majority of consumers get the bulk of their information on environmental matters from the media—primarily television, followed by newspapers, magazines, and radio. A growing percentage are consulting environmental group newsletters and communiques. In 1990, Roper found that 32% of all consumers are exposed to information circulated by environmental groups, representing an important secondary source of consumer information, behind major news media such as TV news and newspapers. (See Exhibit 2.5.)

NEED FOR CONTROL

To help them control a world they increasingly see as risky, green consumers are taking preventive measures like buying natural cleaning products or organic, pesticide-free foods. They are also responding to myriad new consumer buzzwords that signify environmental compati-

EXHIBIT 2.5
Major Sources of Information on Environmental Issues

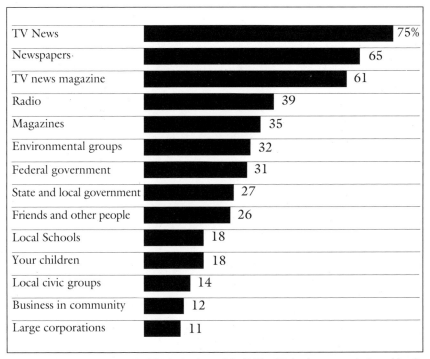

TV News	75%
Newspapers	65
TV news magazine	61
Radio	39
Magazines	35
Environmental groups	32
Federal government	31
State and local government	27
Friends and other people	26
Local Schools	18
Your children	18
Local civic groups	14
Business in community	12
Large corporations	11

Source: *The Environment: Public Attitudes and Individual Behavior*, commissioned by S. C. Johnson & Son, Inc., 1990.

bility such as *recyclable* and *biodegradable* and other terms that now emblazon packages and advertisements. As depicted in Exhibit 2.6, the breadth of buzzwords suggests that green consumers are scrutinizing products at every phase of the lifecycle, from raw material procurement and manufacturing and production, straight through to product "after-use" such as re-use, repair, or recycling, to eventual disposal. It can be hypothesized that after 20 plus years of Naderism, consumers have the wherewithal—or think they do—to put familiar products under a magnifying glass of environmental scrutiny. These buzzwords also suggest that while in-use attributes are of primary importance, consumers' environmental concerns now encompass factors they can't feel or see, such as practices relating to manufacturing, raw materials procurement, and disposal.

EXHIBIT 2.6
The New Purchasing Buzzwords

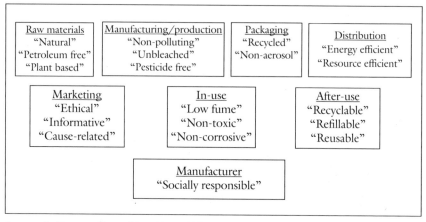

Source: J. Ottman Consulting, Inc., 1992.

Consumer interest in environment-related product purchasing criteria runs deep. For example, almost all (96%) of the respondents in a 1990 poll indicated that environmental criteria factor into their purchasing decisions at least occasionally. As detailed in Exhibit 2.7, upwards of 70% of survey respondents considered attributes such as "energy efficient," "non-polluting," "recyclable," and "ozone-safe" to be most important. Nearly two-thirds of respondents noted "pesticide-free," "biodegradable," "non-corrosive," "non-aerosol," and the ubiquitous "all natural," as well as the now-meaningless "environmentally friendly."

A second control strategy, consumers are patronizing manufacturers and retailers whom they trust. In the absence of complete knowledge about environmental product characteristics, purchasing from trusted manufacturers and retailers provides an added layer of assurance that products are safe. In 1992, Roper found that 34% of the public claimed to avoid products made by specific manufacturers, while 22% claimed to avoid restaurants using plastic foam containers. The potential impact on this for marketers is significant if one considers that this behavior is much more ingrained with Roper's influential True-Blue Greens segment, at 67% and 44%, respectively. (Refer to Exhibit 2.3.) In its much publicized shift away from polystyrene to paper-and-plastic combination hamburger wraps in 1991, McDonalds may have considered the

EXHIBIT 2.7
**The Importance of Environmental Factors
in the Purchase Decision**

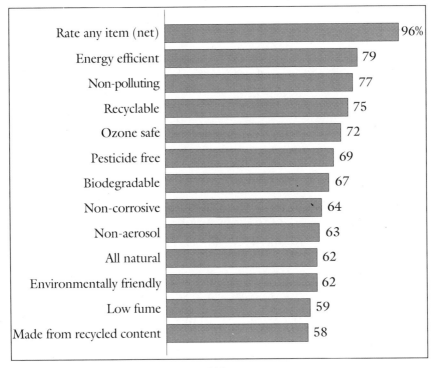

Rate any item (net)	96%
Energy efficient	79
Non-polluting	77
Recyclable	75
Ozone safe	72
Pesticide free	69
Biodegradable	67
Non-corrosive	64
Non-aerosol	63
All natural	62
Environmentally friendly	62
Low fume	59
Made from recycled content	58

Source: Warwick, Baker & Fiore, May 1990.

intense reactions of societal influentials such as the True-Blue Greens, and their potential to sway peers. Indeed, in announcing the move, McDonald's President Edward Rensi declared: "Our consumers just don't feel good about it . . . so we're changing."[13]

NEED TO MAKE A DIFFERENCE

Reflecting a deep-felt need of Baby Boomers to assume responsibility for their actions, green consumers want to feel that they can, if only symbolically, make a difference. It is no coincidence that many best-selling books like *50 Simple Things You Can Do to Save the Earth* use an empowerment theme. A part of this desire stems from the corresponding need to alleviate guilt. While consumers see industry as primarily responsible for

EXHIBIT 2.8
How Societal Groups Rate on Protecting the Environment

	Excellent	Good	Fair	Poor
Environmental groups	14%	46%	30%	7%
Individual Americans	4	26	38	30
Local government	4	25	44	25
State government	3	22	45	27
Private industry	3	17	34	44
Federal government	2	16	40	39

Source: *The Kaagen Environmental Monitor*, 4th Quarter, 1990.

creating environmental ills, they recognize their own culpability as well. For example, when asked to rate various societal groups on how well they protect the environment, consumers rank themselves only slightly better than government and private industry. (See Exhibit 2.8.)

When asked why there isn't more recycling, 34% of consumers in a 1991 poll mentioned "public resistance"—up 8 points in a two-year period, while the number who said "industry is foot dragging" as the main reason has been dropping.[14]

Consumers feel guilty when faced with environmental ills they *can* control but don't. They see themselves as being able to do little about serious environmental problems like global climate change or ozone layer depletion, but as illustrated in Exhibit 2.9, they feel a responsibility to help curb litter, solid waste, indoor air pollution, and air pollution from automobiles.

Everyday behavior such as disposing of what is perceived as excessive packaging and driving gas-guzzlers can serve as daily reminders of personal environmental transgressions. Use of products that are becoming, rightfully or wrongfully, targets of the press—disposable diapers, plastic foam coffee cups, aerosol spray cans, and fur coats—reinforces guilt. Indeed, as shown in Exhibit 2.10, consumers link many of these products with environmental ills. With attitudes so heavily disposed against them, products such as aerosol sprays, disposable diapers, and foam packaging represent prime targets for shifts in consumer purchasing behavior.

EXHIBIT 2.9
How Much Can Individuals Do About
Solving Environmental Problems

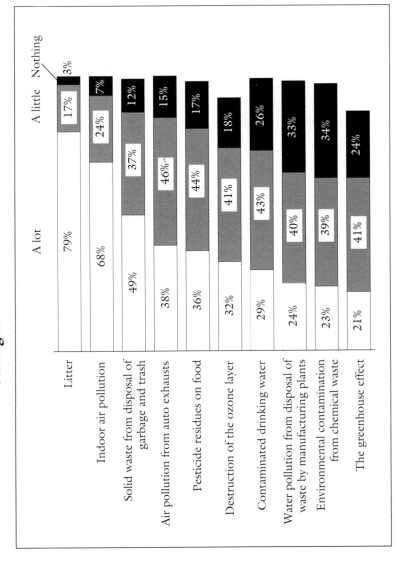

	A lot	A little	Nothing
Litter	79%	17%	3%
Indoor air pollution	68%	24%	7%
Solid waste from disposal of garbage and trash	49%	37%	12%
Air pollution from auto exhausts	38%	46%	15%
Pesticide residues on food	36%	44%	17%
Destruction of the ozone layer	32%	41%	18%
Contaminated drinking water	29%	43%	26%
Water pollution from disposal of waste by manufacturing plants	24%	40%	33%
Environmental contamination from chemical waste	23%	39%	34%
The greenhouse effect	21%	41%	24%

Source: *The Environment: Public Attitudes and Individual Behavior*, The Roper Organization, commissioned by S. C. Johnson & Sons, Inc., 1990.

EXHIBIT 2.10
**Ratings of Products and Packaging Contributing
to Environmental Ills**

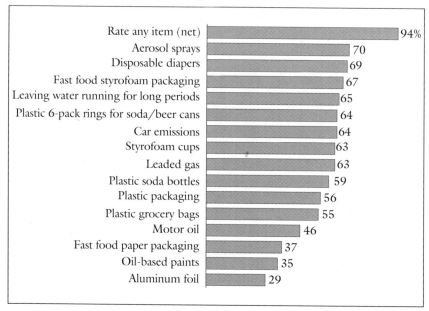

Rate any item (net)	94%
Aerosol sprays	70
Disposable diapers	69
Fast food styrofoam packaging	67
Leaving water running for long periods	65
Plastic 6-pack rings for soda/beer cans	64
Car emissions	64
Styrofoam cups	63
Leaded gas	63
Plastic soda bottles	59
Plastic packaging	56
Plastic grocery bags	55
Motor oil	46
Fast food paper packaging	37
Oil-based paints	35
Aluminum foil	29

Source: Warwick, Baker & Fiore, May 1990.

Polls and empirical data show that consumers are already buying less of those products perceived as environmentally and/or personally harmful; they are switching brands or moving out of brand categories altogether. For example, as of 1992 nearly a third of the total public (28%) claimed to avoid buying aerosols. While polls of this kind tend to overstate behavior, there is in-market evidence that consumers are at least to some extent putting their money where their conscience tells them. For example, following seven straight years of growth, aerosol fillings declined in 1991 for the second year in a row. While fillings were down only 1% in 1990, the decline for 1991 is estimated at a more precipitous 3–5% drop.[15]

Qualitative research suggests that consumers' guilt and desire to make a difference can be manifested in indirect ways. For example, an environmentally aware mother may continue to use disposable diapers despite knowing that they will wind up in a landfill. To assuage her guilt, she may take compensatory steps like going out of her way to recycle the family's bottles, cans, and newspapers (in effect, offsetting the space in the landfill taken up by the diapers). This behavior suggests that consumers each have an environmental repertoire representing the sum total of activities and trade-offs one is willing to make on behalf of the environment. One's environmental repertoire is likely to reflect factors such as age, lifestyle, income, particular environmental interests and concerns, and geographic location, including access to recycling and other after-use/disposal options.

NEED TO MAINTAIN LIFESTYLE

Representing a key challenge for marketers, consumers claim to be willing to do their part, but their behavior indicates they are adverse to making trade-offs in their lifestyles. While this may suggest that they are not committed to environmental cleanup, consumers' willingness to switch brands, and even pay a premium for certain products such as those with a perceived health or quality of life benefit, underscores the opportunity for marketers who can bring technology and imagination to bear on products and communications that project tangible consumer and environmental benefits.

A big difference between today's environmentally aware consumers and their 1970s counterparts is that the latter focused on hard-line, low consumption approaches to environmentalism while the former favors technology-driven solutions that allow them to maintain their lifestyles. The clarion call has changed from "no development" to "sustainable development" with an emphasis on conserving natural resources through smarter management.

Today's consumers recognize that some lifestyle changes are necessary and many are taking steps such as recycling and conserving energy. But, as can be seen in Exhibit 2.3, most consumers express their environmentalism with easy-to-execute behaviors like recycling, while the more inconvenient and time-consuming activities, such as writing to elected officials or cutting down on car use, are regularly practiced by only a small minority: 8% or less. This behavior reflects several factors, prime among them a belief that industry is to blame for the problems and, therefore, should solve them and time constraints.

For example, in 1992 Roper found that 53% of the public say they personally are not doing more for the environment because: "I feel that it's basically large companies which are causing our environmental problems and I think it's these companies, not people like me, who should solve the problems." Slightly less than half of consumers say they are too busy to make lifestyle changes (48%) or to shop around for alternative products (37%).[16]

Although consumers are obviously concerned about the environment, it should come as no surprise that many refuse to trade off on product attributes such as performance, convenience, price, or, in some cases—such as organic foods with their spots and bruises—appearance.

Product efficacy should and will continue to be the primary influence on consumer purchase decisions. After all, one buys a laundry detergent to get clothes clean, not to save the planet. If an environmentally preferable product doesn't meet consumer expectations, it is viewed as a waste of money.

The quest for convenience is legendary in today's marketplace. For the great many working women, and working mothers in particular, short-term, immediate concerns like getting through one's day understandably preempt the longer-term and more remote environmental goals. In addition, consumers want the products they buy to be delivered in a safe, sanitary, and attractive manner. Their desire to buy products with minimal packaging conflicts with their greater needs for safety (e.g., tamperproof lids) and convenience (e.g., microwavable food). The appearance of food signals appetite appeal and purity. This poses a conflict for consumers when forced to choose between organically grown apples with their inconsistent appearance and perfect looking apples ripened with chemicals such as Alar.

As detailed in Exhibit 2.11, Roper has found that, on average, consumers say they would pay a 4.6% price premium for certain types of environmentally sound products. However, this figure includes the Greenback Greens, that very small segment of consumers (5%) who claim to be willing to pay a significant premium (15%+) for environmentally sound products.

Resistance to paying a premium is not surprising. Some consumers simply cannot afford it. Historically, most consumers have not been willing to pay extra money upfront for products that promise a long-term payback, such as energy-efficient refrigerators or light bulbs. Consumers may also equate environmentally sound products with poor value. For example, Roper found that 35-40% of consumers say they are

EXHIBIT 2.11
Average Price Increase Consumers Are Willing to Pay for Green Products

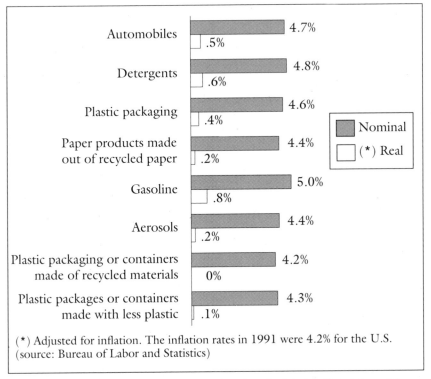

(*) Adjusted for inflation. The inflation rates in 1991 were 4.2% for the U.S. (source: Bureau of Labor and Statistics)

Source: *Environmental Behavior, North America: Canada, Mexico, United States,* The Roper Organization, commissioned by S. C. Johnson & Son, Inc., 1992.

not doing more for the environment because alternative green products are "too expensive" (40%) and "they do not work as well as regular brands (34%).[17] Lack of credibility may also represent a green barrier. A similar number (36%) "do not really believe the labels claiming that a product is environmentally safe."[18] Since they are not aware of the economics associated with bringing some green products to market in the quantities now being demanded, these higher prices may lead consumers to suspect manufacturers of price gouging.

Consumers are however willing to pay a premium—more than 15%—for environmentally sound products that offer a perceived health or quality of life benefit. Products such as organically grown baby foods, natural soft drinks, and unbleached coffee filters command significant price premiums over non-green alternatives. Ask drought-ridden consumers to pay a premium for a water-saving showerhead that replicates the performance of a 7-gallon-per-minute shower and the answer may be a resounding "Yes!"

While environmentally sound product attributes may not always motivate consumers to pay a premium, as pointed out in Chapter 1, research strongly suggests that environmental attributes can act as a powerful tie-breaker and, in general, provide a source of differentiation and added value.

Susan Hayward of Yankelovich, Clancy, Shulman says it best, "Companies who find practical solutions to real problems and make them palatable/believable/understandable to consumers will succeed." Indeed many marketers are finding that consumers will eagerly buy green products that meet their primary needs and that can clearly help to solve an environment-related problem. For example, with broadscale awareness for the need to recycle and preserve our forests, consumers are snapping up household paper products like kitchen towels and bathroom tissue made from recycled content, although up until a few years ago recycled content was rejected as inferior, even unclean. In the future, with a greater awareness of how environmental ills affect health as well as an understanding of the economic factors involved in bringing greener products to market, consumers may be willing to accept greater trade-offs in price or convenience. In the meantime, this suggests opportunities for marketers who can develop easy substitutes to existing products and especially for those who can offer environmentally enhanced versions of popular brands. Other challenges of environmental marketing are discussed in the next chapter.

Notes

1. *Green MarketAlert*, Apr. 1992, p.4.

2. Hayward, Susan, of Yankelovich, Clancy, Shulman, presentation to the American Marketing Association's "Environmental Conference: Green Marketing from a Marketer's Perspective," Oct. 1991.

3. *Environment U.S.A.*, The Angus Reid Group, Toronto, Canada, 1991.

4. Burros, Marian, "Health-Food Superstores? Why, Yes, It's Only Natural," *The New York Times*, Jan. 8, 1992, p.C6.

5. *Ibid.*

6. Adams, Richard, "The Greening of Consumerism," *Journal of Accountancy* (UK), June 1990, p.81.

7. *Ibid.*, p.82.

8. Interview with Willis Harman, "The Role of Business in a Transforming World," *Business Ethics*, Mar.–Apr., 1992, p.28.

9. *Ibid.*, p.29.

10. Cerr, Kevin, "Thinking Green is No Longer Just a Hippy Dream," *Adweek's Marketing Week*, July 9, 1990, p.18.

11. Winski, Joseph, derived from DDB Needham Worldwide, "Life Style Study," *Advertising Age*, Oct. 5, 1990.

12. Alvord, John B., presentation titled "Update on Environmental Labeling and Packaging Regulations: Domestic and Internationally," American Marketing Association's "Environmental Conference: Green Marketing from a Marketer's Perspective," Oct. 1991.

13. Holusha, John, "Packaging and Public Image—McDonald's Fills a Big Order," *The New York Times*, Nov. 2, 1990, p.1.

14. Keller, Edward, The Roper Organization, presentation to the American Marketing Association's "Environmental Conference: Green Marketing from a Marketer's Perspective," Oct. 1991.

15. Carson, Hamilton C., "Chemical Specialties," *Household and Personal Products Industry*, Apr. 1992, p.32.

16. *Environmental Behavior, North America: Canada, Mexico, United States*, The Roper Organization, commissioned by S.C. Johnson & Sons, Inc., 1992.

17. *Ibid.*

18. *Ibid.*

Chapter 3

THE CHALLENGES OF ENVIRONMENTAL MARKETING

Conventional marketing involves providing products that satisfy consumer needs at affordable prices and supporting those products with communications that project value to the consumer. Environmental marketing is more complex and requires new marketing and management strategies that can effectively address key challenges relating to how we define green, how we develop green products that consumers will like, and how we communicate our commitment and initiatives with credibility and impact.

Why Conventional Marketing Won't Work

Environmental marketing serves two key objectives:

• To develop products that balance consumers' needs for performance, affordable pricing, and convenience with *environmental compatibility*, that is, a minimal impact on the environment.

• To project an image of high quality, including *environmental sensitivity*, relating to both a product's attributes and its manufacturer's track record for environmental compliance.

These objectives cannot be met with conventional marketing strategies. Environmental consumerism represents deep psychological and sociological shifts, as did Feminism and Naderism before it. Feminism challenged marketers to develop convenience products and to portray women in advertising with a new respect. Naderism spurred marketers to produce safer, higher-quality products and to support those products with more credible claims. Meeting the challenges of environmental consumerism presents its own new mandates for product development and promotion.

One need only recall the recent backlash from inconsistent and misleading environmental labeling and marketing efforts to realize that conventional strategies won't succeed. Encouraged by polls suggesting that consumers will pay more for green products, marketers rushed headlong to underscore the environmental benefits of their offerings. Indeed, green claims quadrupled between 1989 and 1990.[1] Without regard for many of the challenges of developing and communicating green products, many brands of trash bags and diapers were simply labeled "degradable" and aerosols were tagged as "ozone-friendly." One product was even touted as "earth friendly since 1886." However, the resulting deluge of skepticism, confusion, and regulatory pressures that these green claims spawned quickly proved that environmental marketing involves more than tweaking one or two product attributes and dressing up packages with meaningless claims. Too many marketers learned the hard way that partaking of the many opportunities presented by environmental consumerism requires a thorough commitment to greening both products and communications. As detailed later in this chapter, this commitment needs to be founded on a thorough greening of the company's entire operations.

The Five Challenges of Green
CHALLENGE #1: HOW TO DEFINE GREEN

Green products are typically durable, non-toxic, made from recycled materials, and minimally packaged. Of course, there are no completely green products, for they all use up energy and resources and create waste and pollution during their manufacture, distribution (transportation to warehouses and stores), and afteruse or disposal. So *green* is relative, describing those products with less impact on the environment than alternatives. However, what constitutes green in specific product categories and even areas of the country can vary considerably. Biodegradable may be an appropriate label for laundry detergents, signifying that ingredients decompose in local waterways, but is not appropriate for paper or plastic destined for landfills in which degradation occurs slowly, if at all. Batteries can be considered green if they contain no mercury or other heavy metals, or if they are rechargeable. Green may also vary by region. Solid waste is a critical issue in New Jersey where landfill space is at a premium. Southern California suffers from poor air quality and low water supplies, while Florida's porous soil exacerbates leaching from landfills into underground water. Thus, reusable cloth diapers may be green in the East, where landfill space is at a premium, but may be less desirable in the West.

Frustrated marketers often consider green a moving target. Technology is constantly improving. Consumer attitudes shift, reflecting changes in lifestyles or news of risks associated with established technologies or ingredients. Laws are constantly rewritten accordingly. Thus, what constitutes environmental state-of-the-art today could be obsolete tomorrow.

Back in 1978 in the consumer aerosol industry green meant switching from chlorofluorocarbon (CFC) to hydrocarbon-based propellants to help reduce ozone layer depletion. With new learning suggesting that hydrocarbons create smog when mixed with sunlight, the move is on to find yet another propellant system, like pumps.

Similarly, in the 1970s McDonald's replaced paper hamburger wraps with polystyrene clamshells. Polystyrene helped to keep food hot and uncrushed. McDonald's liked the fact that polystyrene cost less than paper. From an environmental standpoint, polystyrene utilized a petroleum waste product. At the time, however, neither plastics nor landfills were consumer issues. Times changed. Polystyrene became associated with ozone depleting CFC-blowing agents, overflowing landfills, and littered highways. Despite aggressive efforts to recycle polystyrene and to educate consumers on the fact that foamed polystyrene was no longer blown with CFCs, McDonald's was forced to replace the polystyrene container. In 1991 it introduced a paper-and-plastic combination wrap that is 20% lighter than polystyrene and significantly less voluminous. Although it is not technically recyclable like polystyrene, quilt rap helps to slow down the newly perceived environmental problem of rapidly closing landfills.

Defining green is even more challenging because no agreed upon method exists to measure the precise relative environmental impacts of a product against alternatives. For example, it is difficult to measure the relative environmental impacts of paper versus cloth towels. As explained in greater detail in Chapter 5, life cycle assessment can detect areas for improvement among similar products, but is not able to yield clear-cut answers as to which of two products is more environmentally sound.

CHALLENGE #2: HOW TO ENLIST CONSUMER SUPPORT FOR LIFESTYLE CHANGES NECESSARY FOR GREENER BEHAVIOR AND PRODUCTS

While green products can often be less costly, more convenient, or perform better than alternatives, at times, they can also be less sanitary, less efficient, and less convenient. For example, ceramic or glass bathroom cups harbor germs, while paper cups, used only once, do not. Household cleaning products like Lysol contain synthetic chemicals, but they disinfect better than alternative cleaning products like baking soda. Detergents with phosphates can get clothes looking cleaner than detergents without. Similarly, taking mass transportation is often less convenient than driving, and sorting the trash requires more effort than not. Consumer reluctance to make tradeoffs in lifestyles and product purchasing challenges marketers to develop products that balance primary needs with environmental compatibility and educating consumers on the need to make changes in their lifestyles in cases where this is not possible.

CHALLENGE #3: HOW TO OVERCOME MISPERCEPTIONS AND BALANCE ENVIRONMENTAL ILLS WITH SOLUTIONS

Many environmental ills evoke terror scenarios: holes in the ozone layer, overflowing landfills, hypodermic needles washing up on beaches—it all sounds very frightening. However, by virtue of their viscerality, these dramatic images can distort consumers' perceptions of what constitutes a real threat to personal health, the environment, or both. As described in Chapter 4, misperceptions can detract from focusing on real issues and lead to unproductive public-policy making. They can also pose significant risks to industry, forcing unnecessary and costly changes in products and manufacturing processes.

For example, media coverage of the link between CFC-propelled aerosol sprays and ozone layer depletion seems to have left an indelible impression on consumers' minds. Much to the dismay of manufacturers of aerosol-packaged products, 12 years after the 1978 ban on ozone-depleting CFCs, more than half of all Americans still believe that aerosols contain CFCs and 60% blame aerosols for holes in the ozone layer. Consumers rank aerosols second only to styrofoam containers as "packages that should be replaced."[2]

Landfills may represent more of an environmental issue than an environmental ill. For example, consumers are not aware that modern technology such as plastic liners for landfills can prevent seepage that would otherwise contaminate underground water. Thus, lingering negative associations of landfills, the not in my backyard (NIMBY) sentiment, not lack of space, prevents further landfills from being sited.

CHALLENGE #4: HOW TO COMMUNICATE WITHOUT UNIFORM GUIDELINES FOR ENVIRONMENTAL MARKETING TERMS

Commonly used environmental marketing terms can mean many things and as such can mislead unsuspecting, uninformed consumers. For example, products or packaging made from recycled content can be crafted from 10% recycled content or 100% recycled content. Recycled content can include pre-consumer recycled material, such as factory trimmings, or post-consumer content, such as used milk jugs and newspapers. A package may be recyclable in theory, but collection facilities may not be available to consumers in their communities.

Complicating the issue, there are currently no nationally accepted guidelines for using environmental marketing claims for advertising and product labeling. As of July 1992, the FTC has issued voluntary guidelines for environmental marketing terms. However, these guidelines are not legally enforceable, and many states have already passed their own labeling laws, which are not preempted by the FTC's guidelines. Eleven states including California, Rhode Island, and New York have already adopted legislation defining terms such as recycled, recyclable, and reusable. However, these guidelines are not consistent across the states, prohibiting the use of one label for nationally distributed brands. This has prompted a number of marketers of major national brands including Kraft General Foods, Heinz, and Andrew Jergens to stop using claims such as ''contains recycled content'' and ''recyclable'' on product labels.

This lack of consistency among industry, government, and the scientific community is confusing consumers and is creating an uneven playing field. According to J. Walter Thompson, only 20% of Americans describe their understanding of environmental issues as "very good." When probed on specific environmental terms, 64% of consumers are not confident about the term biodegradable, while 34% are not confident they know what recyclable means.[3] Without a mechanism for understanding and communicating the relative environmental impacts of all market entries, and an overload of potential cases of misleading claims before regulators, marketers risk losing business to products that are wrongfully touted as green. For example, pressure from consumers and retailers to keep up with competitive degradable entries—and the threat of losing significant market share—prompted Mobil to introduce its own degradable trash bag in 1989. Mobil introduced its degradable bags despite earlier pronouncements that degradability was not a solution to solid waste management,[4] triggering a backlash described later in this chapter.

Lack of uniform guidelines also poses risks to marketers who cannot communicate their greenness in the face of legitimate, often regionally based, competition.

CHALLENGE #5: HOW TO GAIN CREDIBILITY AND ASSERT THAT THE INTERESTS OF INDUSTRY DO NOT CONFLICT WITH GREENNESS

Industry is seen as creating the bulk of all pollution and controlling most of the natural resources, but is not perceived as having the necessary incentives to prevent further pollution or encourage cleanup. This has resulted in low credibility for industry's environment-related messages and a backlash is already in place. Environmental disasters such as the Bhopal tragedy and the Exxon Valdez oil spill may only have served to underscore consumers' perception of industry as reckless and uncaring. Only 7% of Americans believe companies are taking the appropriate steps to protect the environment and 58% are unable to name a single company they consider to be "environmentally friendly."[5] The chemical (71%), and oil and gas (70%) industries are viewed as among the most environmentally careless industries, followed by plastics (69%), household cleaning products (65%), and agricultural chemicals (62%). (See Exhibit 3.1.)

Compounding the issues, manufacturers of consumer products historically have been viewed as being in the business of selling more, not less. To consumers, product obsolescence has long represented an industry plot to promote consumption; advertising sells goods that consumers do not want. Perceived manufacturer self-interest represents a barrier to the ultimate credibility of industry. The issue is described by one environmentalist this way:

> But all the *50 Simple Things* (a book on consumer-directed environmental tips) in the world aren't going to make an appreciable dent in our resource abuse until some meaningful changes occur in behavior and lifestyle. And this is where green marketing generally falls on its face: it will never disclose the full range of options. The recycled paper towel package will never shout "Go buy a sponge!" The ozone-friendly Gillette shaving cream can will never advise green consumers to switch to a shaving bar. Green marketing will never offer a well-rounded "third E" (referring to the role of industry in Educating consumers on how to solve environmental ills).[6]

Industry's dearth of credibility in communicating on environmental issues is illustrated in a 1991 poll conducted by The Angus Reid Group, in which consumers were asked to rate the credibility of various sources of environmental information. Business executives and industry associations received the lowest credibility ratings of all sources by far—only 37% said they believe most or some of what these representatives have to say about matters. (See Exhibit 3.2.)

No doubt a reflection of the raft of confusing claims that have been put forth, almost half of all adults (45%) believe only some or none of today's green product claims.[7]

A backlash is in place among consumers and the media who are quick to broadcast any industry misstep. The FTC and individual states have already settled several cases and are reviewing dozens of others.

In the most publicized such case, the Mobil Oil Corporation was sued for use of deceptive advertising and consumer fraud by 7 states for its use of the term degradable. As mentioned above, in June 1989, Mobil introduced a reformulated version of its Hefty trash bags with

EXHIBIT 3.1
Selected Industrial Sectors' Public Image for Environmental Consciousness

	Very Careless (%)	A Little Careless (%)	A Little Careful (%)	Very Careful (%)	(Unsure) (%)	Industrial Concern Index
Environmentally Conscious Sectors:						
Glass and Bottle Industry	7	26	43	11	12	+21
Electricity Utilities	9	27	41	11	11	+16
Banks and Other Financial Institutions	9	24	34	9	24	+10
Hospitals and Health Care Facilities	14	29	37	12	8	+6
Newspaper Industry	11	32	36	7	14	0
Careless Sectors:						
Retail Stores	11	33	32	4	20	−9
Nuclear Energy Industry	22	28	27	14	9	−9
Public Transportation Services	13	40	33	5	9	−15
Quick Service Restaurants	21	35	34	5	5	−17
Forestry and Pulp & Paper Companies	20	36	28	7	9	−21
Waste Management Industry	21	36	27	8	8	−22
Automobile Manufacturers	21	37	30	6	7	−22
Cosmetic Manufacturers	17	33	22	5	23	−23
Packaged Goods Industry	18	39	29	5	9	−23
Environmentally Dangerous Sectors:						
Mining Industry	24	33	22	5	17	−30
Agricultural Chemical Industry	23	39	25	5	8	−32
Household Cleaning Product Manufacturers	24	41	22	4	8	−38
Plastics Industry	31	38	21	3	7	−45
Oil and Gas Companies	39	31	19	5	5	−45
Chemical Industry	34	37	18	4	6	−49

*The Industrial Concern Index is derived by subtracting the proportion of respondents describing a sector as environmentally "careless" from the proportion describing it as "careful." Therefore, the higher the number, the better a sector's reputation for environmental consciousness. Conversely, a negative number means more people view that sector as "careless" than "careful," and the size of the number depicts the magnitude of the discrepancy.

Source: *Environment U.S.A.*, The Angus Reid Group, Toronto, Canada, 1991.

EXHIBIT 3.2
Sources and Credibility of Environmental Information Sources

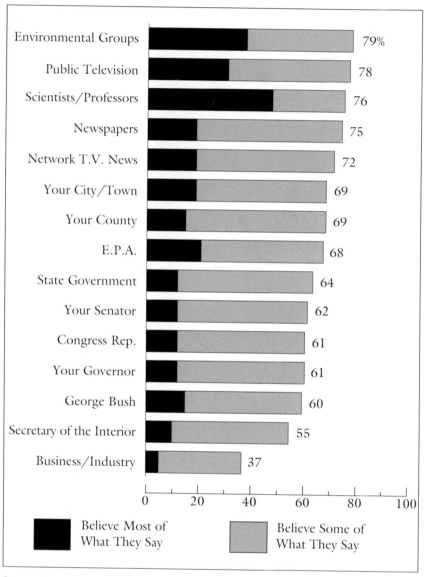

Source: *Environment U.S.A.*, The Angus Reid Group, 1991.

an additive designed to trigger degradation when exposed to the sun. To announce the change, Hefty boxes featured a pine tree and sunbeam with an eagle. The term degradable was prominent but included the explanation: "Activated by exposure to the elements." The back of the box provided further explanation of the new technology. Within 6 months of its introduction, Hefty trash bags and other brands of degradable trash bags were under fire. Research conducted by garbologists who study landfills (where most of the trash bags and their contents would wind up) revealed that garbage deposited in landfills is not exposed to sunlight or other elements required to begin the degradation process. Environmentalists brought this fact to the public, setting off the case against Mobil. Stating that Mobil's advertising claims "break down faster than their garbage bags," the state Attorneys General maintained that given current disposal options, the product didn't work as claimed. The case was settled with Mobil having to pay significant fines and becoming a lasting symbol of consumer environmental deception in the process.

In another example, Procter & Gamble, the manufacturers of Pampers and Luvs disposable diapers, ran a national print ad discussing its commitment to composting and the potential for composting as a solid waste management solution for diapers. Regulators in New York State questioned the accuracy of claims made in the ads. They maintained that advertising led consumers to believe that Pampers and Luvs could be composted in New York when in fact the infrastructure for commercial composting of this type did not exist there. P&G added disclaimers in subsequent advertising.

Despite a reputation for pro-active environmentalism, Du Pont invited criticism upon broadcasting a television commercial heralding its Conoco Oil subsidiary's decision to switch to double-hulled oil tankers. While many environmentalists supported the decision, environmental group Friends of the Earth did not. In a 112-page report, the group praised Du Pont for its commitment but made it clear that proclaiming the company as a friend to nature as displayed in the advertising was premature. They outlined the company's environmental transgressions and concluded with recommendations for Du Pont to truly befriend the earth.[8]

The Ultimate Challenge: Organizing for Green Success

If many marketers' activities conducted in the early days of the environmental consumerism movement (1988–1991) taught us anything, it is that consumers' concerns cannot be exploited through superficial product improvements and/or communications. Environmental issues represent questions of survival for millions of people around the world. As demonstrated time and again, consumer retaliation—as well as that from environmentalists, regulators, and the media—against companies who they feel are exploiting the environment can be serious, swift, and enduring.

Potentially representing the greatest challenge of all, marketers who aim to develop and market environmentally sound products successfully in the 1990s must first *prove* their environmental credentials. It is not enough to talk green, companies must *be* green. Far from the communications-only issue that many marketers originally perceived, successfully addressing consumers' environmental concerns requires a thorough greening that extends deep into corporate culture. It is only through the creation and implementation of strong, deeply valued environmental policies that more environmentally sound products and services can be developed. And, it is only through the creation of a corporate-wide environmental ethic that sincere consumer-responsive marketing strategies and communications efforts can be executed.

Many companies have already begun to take substantive steps to green their operations, bring their employees on board, and communicate their initiatives to all corporate stakeholders. They are finding that such greening not only pays off in exciting new green products, but helps them to save money, improve employee morale, recruit more productively, and keep their shareholders happy.

Following are nine strategies for preparing your company to effectively meet the challenges of environmental consumerism and take advantage of its many opportunities.

GET YOUR HOUSE IN ORDER

Hubert H. "Skip" Humphrey III, State Attorney General of Minnesota and principal author of *Green Report II*, said it best: "Green your operations and the products will take care of themselves. 'Green' your products and the marketing will take care of itself."[9]

Companies looking to engage in environmental marketing need to start by preparing themselves: by doing their homework to understand the full range of environmental, consumer, economic, and political issues that affect their business and addressing them with integrity. When this preparation is in place, a company is most ready to take advantage of the opportunities while minimizing the potential for controversy.

Many consumer product manufacturers embark on internal greening efforts with a full environmental audit performed by an independent environmental engineering firm.

BE PRO-ACTIVE

Because what is considered green today may not be considered green tomorrow, get out *ahead of the curve*. By being pro-active companies stand the best chance of finding cost-effective solutions to environmental ills, and getting a head start on competitors in meeting regulations and consumer expectations. Southern California Edison, for example, has already pledged a 20% reduction in carbon dioxide emissions by 2010. By getting an early start, the company can take the steps that represent the least cost to its customers.

Recognizing that a pro-active approach is necessary to help define the standards by which they will be judged and establish credibility with consumers, the policies and products of many leading-edge companies often go far beyond regulatory compliance: they are setting standards for their industries. These companies are likely to win kudos from consumers, environmentalists, and the media for their innovativeness and commitment. Monsanto, for one, has pledged to cut toxic air emissions by 90% in 1992 and then work towards a goal of 0% toxic air emissions. AT&T plans to phase out CFC use by the end of 1994, to reduce waste from manufacturing processes by 25% and paper use by 15%, and to achieve a 35% paper recycling rate. By the end of 1995, it expects to cut toxic air emissions by 95%.[10]

Voluntarily going beyond regulatory compliance often generates cost savings. Indeed, the benefits of adopting environmentally sound business strategies are making many consumer product companies change the way they think about managing environmental issues. For example, many are discovering that waste is not necessarily a useless by-product that is costly to dispose of, but rather represents a *misused* resource that can help save money. Chapter 5 includes several examples of how using recycled content or eliminating packaging saves money that can be passed along to consumers. 3M provides an excellent example of this new thinking and how it can bring about exciting new consumer products as well.

3M: Where Pollution Prevention Pays Big Dividends

In 1975, the St. Paul, Minnesota-based 3M, manufacturer of industrial and consumer products including Scotchguard fabric protector and Scotch tape, realized that pending stiff environmental regulations would eventually force them to reduce significantly the pollution from their manufacturing plants. Rather than proceed with conventional—and costly—end-of-the-pipe pollution control methods, such as installing smokestack scrubbers, 3M decided to pursue the concept of source reduction. That is, to reduce emissions *before* they were created. They believed that this strategy would cut costs and put the company in a stronger competitive position long term. They were right.

As part of a corporate-wide program called Pollution Prevention Pays (3P), 3M overhauled its product formulations and manufacturing processes to eliminate completely many types of emissions. Through strategies such as redesigning production equipment and recycling manufacturing by-products for use in other processes, between 1975 and 1989 the 3P program saved 3M over $500 million. It has spared the environment more than 500,000 tons of pollutants, and has saved a 1.6 billion gallons of wastewater. Current goals (based on 1987 initial levels) by the year 2000 include reducing hazardous and nonhazardous releases to air, water, and land by 90%, and reducing waste by 50% by the year 2000. The company has even sold recycled manufacturing by-products to other companies.

What started out as an internal greening program focused on persuading employees that there was value in getting out ahead of the regulatory curve is regarded by environmentalists and media as an outstanding environmental effort. The recipient of many awards including the President's 1991 Environment and Conservation Challenge Award, the 3P program has helped to establish a reputation for 3M as a leading-edge corporate environmentalist.

The environmental culture that now permeates 3M is beginning to pay off in exciting new products that address consumers' environmental concerns, while pre-empting competition and legislation. Some recent 3M innovations include: Safest Stripper paint and varnish remover, the first water-based paint stripper that effectively eliminates the risks associated with methylene chloride (a suspected carcinogen); and environmentally improved versions of existing products such as Scotchguard fabric protector with no CFCs and limited trichloroethylene and Post-it note pads using recycled paper.[11]

START WITH A TOP DOWN COMMITMENT

With consumers scrutinizing products at every phase of the life cycle, leading-edge companies recognize that corporate greening must extend to every department. The effort must bring together marketing, research and development, production, package design, consumer and public affairs, and environmental staffs. Only senior management can add the necessary weight to the message for all employees and other environmental stakeholders to realize that the corporation truly cares and that environmental soundness is indeed a priority.

From an image standpoint, the need to start with the Chief Executive Officer cannot be over-emphasized. The consumer backlash against Exxon over the 1989 oil spill in Alaska's Prince William Sound may have been caused as much by CEO Lawrence Rawls' delayed appearance on the scene as it was by outrage over the environmental degradation that resulted. In the age of environmental consumerism, leading-edge companies such as The Body Shop and Tom's of Maine, described later in this book, are winning consumers' trust by projecting a personal commitment usually in the form of the CEO. From a marketing standpoint, corporate personalities can help to create a personal and emotional link between the brand and the company that makes it. A personality can act as a symbolic police officer who is watching over corporate operations and ensuring environmental compliance. CEOs are believable because they are perceived as having a personal stake in the outcome. Not necessarily limited to small companies, as described below, Richard Mahoney of Monsanto is making a strong case for CEOs as "Chief Environmental Officers."

EMPOWER EMPLOYEES

Utilize education and incentive programs to empower employees to develop more environmentally sound processes and products. When employees are aware of the issues and given the authority to make changes, environmentally sound products and practices will be developed. At Coca-Cola, all employees participate in an Environmental Development Program. This one-and-one-half hour video program discusses many of the myths and realities of environmental issues and outlines Coca-Cola's accomplishments. All employees are reminded that environmental issues are not the sole responsibility of the Environmental Affairs Department, but rather that everyone needs to be involved every day. Program participants receive a certificate and pin. Reports one company executive, "Employees love it. They want to know that the company cares."[12]

APPROACH "GREENING" AS A CONTINUOUS PROCESS

Skip Humphrey has described environmental marketing as a race without a finish line. Because definitive answers to the questions of green are not always available and overall environmental excellence is a desirable but not realistic goal, corporate environmentalism should be viewed as a series of small steps on the learning curve. Companies on the leading edge of corporate environmentalism take an inventory of emissions and waste, develop a plan, set measurable goals, and work towards them. They constantly integrate, learn, and refine their products and processes.

BE THOROUGH

Environmental initiatives must be undertaken all throughout the company, not just confined to the factory. As 3M has discovered, cutting down waste all over the company, such as recycling measures in the office, helps to motivate all employees to help create more environmentally enhanced products and services, more relevant communications, and better customer relations.

The Monsanto Pledge

Monsanto, a $9 billion per year chemical company, is proving the value of employee empowerment in developing outstanding environmental programs that make a difference and build credibility. In setting his company on an environmental course in 1990, CEO Richard Mahoney created the Monsanto Pledge—a pledge to be environmentally responsible by reducing emissions, eliminating waste, working for sustainable agriculture, and managing corporate land to benefit nature. (See Exhibit 3.3.) Realizing that the Monsanto Pledge wouldn't be effective without the commitment and participation of his 40,000 employees, Mahoney invited colleagues to sign the pledge as well. The company sent out poster-sized pledges for employees to sign and made up wallet-sized replicas. The company also instituted a Monsanto Awards Program to recognize employees for their environmental efforts. As many as four annual awards of $25,000 each go to environmental organizations chosen by award recipients.

Monsanto employees are appropriately empowered to initiate environmental projects. For example, at the Soda Springs, Idaho, plant em-

EXHIBIT 3.3
The Monsanto Pledge

*T*he Monsanto Pledge is our vision of environmental responsibility. It shapes the on-the-job decisions of every Monsanto employee worldwide and guides the company in achieving its overall commitment to meaningful environmental, safety and health solutions.

It is our pledge to:

Reduce all toxic and hazardous releases and emissions, working toward an ultimate goal of zero effect;

Ensure no Monsanto operation poses any undue risk to our employees and our communities;

Work to achieve sustainable agriculture through new technology and practices;

Ensure groundwater safety;

Keep our plants open to our communities and involve the community in plant operations;

Manage all corporate real estate, including plant sites, to benefit nature; and

Search worldwide for technology to reduce and eliminate waste from our operations, with the top priority being not making it in the first place.

Source: Monsanto, January 1990. Reprinted with permission from Monsanto.

ployees developed a reforestation program that is being replicated elsewhere, and colleagues at the St. Louis headquarters are creating waste-reduction programs for their trash. Office workers organized a recycling committee that, thus far, has recycled more than 3,800 tons of white office paper.

Diane Herndon, public relations manager at Monsanto, reports on how the employee environmental spirit is paying off for the company:

> The environmental programs have really been contagious. They create an impetus that takes on a life of its own. And by staying ahead of the regulatory curve, we can improve the environment our way. We can unleash employee creativity and enthusiasm. Employees really embrace the company's environmental goals, and they can embrace them in a way that makes sense for them.[13]

According to Herndon, the pledge serves as the company's vision of environmental responsibility and it reports on achievements towards pledge goals in an Environmental Annual Review that gives employees and the public a way to track the company's progress.

COMMUNICATE IT

Above all, the environmental consumerism trend is about saving people. The consumer doesn't need another widget packaged in a recycled content box. The consumer needs to breathe fresh air, drink clean water, and feel secure that his/her children will be able to do the same. So companies need to project a clear, earnest message that they genuinely *care* about the health and well-being of consumers and they are constantly integrating the environmental concerns into their products and processes. In other words, when it comes to environmental performance, it is not enough for a company to simply assert a strong commitment to environmental cleanup and preservation; it must be publicly accountable and viewed as continuously improving its environmental performance.

As interest in the *Shopping for a Better World* guidebook suggests, consumers want to know who they're buying from. The guidebook helps to demystify the manufacturers behind the products, providing consumers with a peek inside. Recognizing this, many companies are establishing credibility and building relationships with their consumers by opening the doors—conducting plant tours, disclosing information honestly and clearly, and beefing up their consumer hotlines.

In Germany, chemical manufacturers recognized that the mysterious nature of their manufacturing plants created suspicion among community residents. To help overcome the fear that resulted, manufacturers embarked on an openness campaign, conducting plant tours for local residents and interested parties. In the United States and Canada, chemical manufacturers such as Dow Chemical and Polaroid are utilizing similar openness strategies as part of an industry-wide program entitled Responsible Care. Seeking to re-establish credibility and bring the industry's image more in line with consumer expectations, the Responsible Care program has set out a code of standards and practices in the areas of health, safety, and the environment, and requires member companies to establish objectives, develop strategies and action plans, and start monitoring and reporting progress to the public—good or bad.

Contrary to what many in industry have thought in the past, public disclosure of information is not to be feared as a competitive disadvantage or an invitation to litigation; its benefits outweigh the risks. As noted by Art Kleiner writing in the *Harvard Business Review:*

> The Emergency Planning and Right to Know Provision (Title III) of the Superfund Amendments and Reauthorization Act that since 1986 has required companies to report their emission levels of 300 hazardous chemicals, has resulted in very few citizen group protests or even requests for more information. People chiefly want to be kept informed. The public will accept reasonable progress.[14]

PROJECT YOUR VALUES

In the words of Roy Spence, President of Austin-based GSD&M advertising, in the 1990s ". . . what you stand for will be just as important as what you sell." Most companies currently seek to do a minimum to meet regulatory compliance. A slightly larger number tend to exceed regulatory compliance when prompted by economic benefits. Few are the companies that are motivated by a value system that places a premium on environmental and social wherewithal. These companies are likely to have been founded to promote a system of values beyond or in addition to profits. Thus, they are often willing to pursue environmental and social initiatives at the expense of short-term profits. The companies in this category are usually small, young, and entrepreneurial. Because of their innovative social and environmental policies and practices, they are in the lead in capturing the attention of customers and the media on environmental issues. As a result of their visibility, these deep green companies are raising the expectations of consumers while raising the ante for all corporations. It is these companies who are, in effect, defining many of the rules of corporate environmentalism and social responsibility by which all companies are increasingly being judged and in which all may ultimately be forced to operate.

While many of these values-based companies are small and can be easily dismissed as fringe companies, keep in mind that consumers hold high expectations for larger corporations. As the manufacturers of established national brands, they have more at stake, too. In order to effectively compete in a rapidly changing business environment, larger companies will need to project their values in a similarly convincing manner. To do so, they will need creativity and the ability to think big.

The Body Shop is just one example of a small, values-based company that is winning the respect of consumers through innovative thinking and policies. Indeed, many of today's principles of environmental marketing are being defined by this company's CEO, Anita Roddick. Marketers large and small can learn much from her example.

The Body Shop

The Body Shop is a specialty retail chain of all natural cosmetics and toiletries that was founded in the United Kingdom in 1976 by Anita Roddick. The company's astonishing growth reflects marketing techniques that Roddick believes best meet her customers' needs as both consumers and environmentally caring world citizens. Roddick's company now stands at the forefront of marketers who are benefitting from growing environmental consciousness. Starting with one store outside of London, The Body Shop now has more than 700 outlets in 41 countries; 84 outlets are in the United States. What makes The Body Shop unique from all other cosmetics marketers is its emphasis on consumer empowerment and social values.

Roddick uses mostly natural ingredients in her cosmetics and never tests her products on animals. Ingredients are largely plant-based, thus helping to stay low on the food chain. Consumers can buy in various quantities—Roddick believes that consumers should not be forced to buy more than they need. Depending upon local restrictions, consumers can bring their plastic bottles back for refills or recycling. Whenever possible, ingredients are sourced in developing countries, reflecting Roddick's belief that economies are best stimulated by "trade not aid." Anita Roddick regularly travels to remote regions of the world in search of natural oils, muds, and production methods. The Body Shop's prominently displayed literature details product ingredients and reassures consumers of wholesomeness.

The chain insists on sincere commitments to social issues from its employees. The Body Shop's environmental ethic helps motivate employees and franchise owners who tend to believe strongly in the firm and its products. There are no artsy product promotions in window displays—environmental causes are showcased instead. Store personnel spend approximately one half-day per week on company time doing volunteer social service in their local trading area. In 1990, Roddick took a truck convoy and 30 volunteers to Romania to clean and repair orphanages.

Roddick makes it easy for consumers to feel good about shopping at The Body Shop. Products and packaging may be simplified, but are inherently appealing. Perhaps even more unusual, her messages shun discussions of the superiority of her products or the results of using them. Believing that beauty is more than skin deep, she refuses to present the idealized images of attractive product users touted by other cosmetic marketers.

The results have been nothing short of extraordinary. The Body Shop has grown at a double digit rate for the past 6 years. In 1991, annual sales reached $196 million with an estimated $34 million pre-tax profit. The company is positioned for future growth; the emphasis on inherent values has attracted a loyal following among young upscale women—

tomorrow's major cosmetics buyers. With this group as a base, The Body Shop is poised to achieve its goal of opening approximately 1,200 stores in the United States over the next 10 years.

According to *Business Week*, "Roddick has rewritten the rules for the $16 billion global cosmetics business."[15] Indeed, Roddick's success has spurred major U.S. marketers such as Avon, Revlon, Mary Kay, and Estee Lauder to introduce natural cosmetics lines of their own. They have also joined the ranks of companies with product lines that are cruelty-free. ⊕

TURN YOUR BRAND MANAGERS INTO BRAND STEWARDS

A new approach to marketing management can help consumer product companies address the challenges of environmental marketing and take best advantage of its opportunities: environmental brand stewardship. Compared to conventional brand managers, brand stewards manage their brands for environmental impact as well as for profit and are responsible for communicating their brand's environmental compatibility so as to enhance its overall image and strengthen its competitiveness. Brand stewards assume a proactive stance, striving to go beyond regulatory compliance to meet consumers' expectations for health protection and preservation of the environment. They take a long-term view of their businesses, making provisions for advantages in technology or shortages in natural resources that could adversely affect their profits. They closely monitor regional environmental issues and are quick to address opportunities in particular markets and regions. They assume responsibility for their product's environmental impact, from cradle to grave.

Many chemical companies are now practicing a concept called product stewardship. According to Jon Plaut, director of environmental compliance at Allied Signal, "Product responsibility, or product stewardship, deals with all areas that go into the making, designing, distributing, and marketing of a product. Our Product Responsibility Program covers the entire process from new product review, to design review, to reliability review, to process and product literature, to transportation, to customer complaints, to product recall."[16] However, with the help

EXHIBIT 3.4
Perspective on Brand Stewardship

Brand Management		*Brand Stewardship*
Brand Group	➡	Interdisciplinary Environmental Team
Short-Term	➡	Long-Term
National	➡	Regional
Product End Benefits	➡	Cradle-to-Grave
Selling Benefits	➡	Communicating Values
Manufacturer & Agencies	➡	New Coalitions

of an interdisciplinary team, brand stewardship encompasses these same responsibilities but goes one step further: it recognizes the specific implications of environmental issues for product branding. Beyond product performance, brand managers have traditionally been responsible for creating the distinctive images that add value to and differentiate one product from another. In developing relevant brand images in the age of environmental consumerism, brand stewards communicate specific values beyond sheer product benefits. They strive to create a relationship with their customers that goes beyond the opaque, to where a brand's image is all that matters, to the transparent, so that consumers can see beyond a brand to its manufacturer. In doing so, they enlist the support of organizations such as environmental and regulatory groups as much needed complements to their advertising and public relations agencies.

Environmental brand stewardship affords marketers the opportunity to assume a more strategic role within their companies. Brand stewards develop positive relationships with all corporate environmental stakeholders (including governmental, environmental groups, retailers, the media, and even children who influence their parents' purchasing decisions and represent future customers). They are responsible for incorporating their responses into corporate and product planning. Some progressive companies are already practicing brand stewardship principles. At Coca-Cola, for example, all business reviews must include an environmental impact statement.[17]

With houses in order and armed with an appreciation for the challenges of environmental marketing, marketers are ready to make the most of the many opportunities available in this new marketing age. Capturing the many opportunities and addressing the challenges they create will require as a first step that industry enlist the support of consumers and all corporate environmental stakeholders. Strategies for accomplishing this are detailed in the following chapter.

Notes

1. *Greenwatch*, No.3, J. Walter Thompson, Spring/Summer 1991.

2. *Household and Personal Products Industry*, April 1992, p.71.

3. *Greenwatch*, No.3, J. Walter Thompson, Spring/Summer 1991.

4. Lawrence, Jennifer, "Mobil Case Study," *Advertising Age*, Jan. 1991, p.12.

5. "Findings on Environmental Issues," *Decision Research*, Mar. 1991, and Warwick, Baker & Fiore Advertising, May, 1990.

6. Letter to J. Ottman from Hannah Holmes, Associate Editor, *Garbage*, March 13, 1992.

7. *Greenwatch*, No.3, J. Walter Thompson, Spring/Summer 1991.

8. Holmes, Paul, "Green Has Run More Than Skin Deep," *Inside PR*, Feb. 1992, p.26.

9. Humphrey, Hubert H. III, General Electric Environmental Symposium, Oct. 9, 1991.

10. Brown, Lester, *et al.*, *State of the World, 1992*. Worldwatch Institute, 1992, p.184.

11. Company literature and telephone conversations with M. Virgintino, 3M, and *Discount Merchandiser,* Feb. 1992, p.76.

12. Telephone conversation with Deborah Cross, Coca-Cola Co., May 5, 1992.

13. *Business Ethics*, MA, 1992, p.31.

14. Kleiner, Art, "What Does It Mean To Be Green?" *Harvard Business Review*, Jul.–Aug. 1991, p.42.

15. Zinn, Laura, "Whales, Human Rights, Rainforests, and the Heady Smell of Profits." *Business Week*, July 15, 1991.

16. Plaut, Jon, "Making the Global Playing Field Level," *Marketing: What's New, What's Next,* The Conference Board, reprint number 966, p.24.

17. Schlossberg, Howard, "Marketers Say State Laws Hurt Their Green Efforts," *Marketing News,* Nov. 11, 1991.

Chapter 4

ENLISTING THE SUPPORT OF ENVIRONMENTAL STAKEHOLDERS

To leverage the opportunities of environmental consumerism, marketers must aim at a new green target: corporate environmental stakeholders. Conventional marketing focuses on the consumer. However, consumers' purchasing decisions and industry's operating climate are increasingly being influenced by a number of societal groups that have a stake in corporate policies and practices. Enlisting their support can lead to balanced legislation, continued markets for products and added credibility, among other benefits.

The Environmental Stakeholders

Environmental stakeholders extend beyond the obvious corporate stakeholders of employees, investors, and suppliers to include legislators and government agencies, educators, environmentalists, retailers, the media, and children. There is as much to gain from enlisting their support as there is to lose if they are ignored.

Skepticism over marketers' green claims and distrust of activities viewed as "greenwashing" have made consumers turn to environmentalists and the media for information on the issues. However, their messages can sometimes be misguided, one-sided, conflicting, or otherwise inadequate. Legislation and regulations are not always well-founded or comprehensive. Misperceptions abound about the environmental impacts of industry's practices and processes. This all represents the potential for lost sales, tarnished reputations, and future backlash against industry.

Marketers can't afford to lose their stakeholders' support. While the burden of solving environmental problems rests on industry as the primary polluters, developing workable solutions requires the concerted efforts of industry and *all* of its stakeholders. Take recycling. For recycling to be successful, government must develop a collection system, industry needs to incorporate used materials into new products, and consumers must purchase these products. To protect its markets, safeguard its reputation, and bring about balanced solutions to environmental problems, industry needs to be its own green spokesperson and enter into a dialogue with environmental stakeholders. These efforts represent a unique opportunity for industry to demonstrate leadership and develop win-win strategies.

Communicating credibly and building coalitions with diverse environmental stakeholders is challenging. Industry's management skills are tried and tested, but forging relationships—or building coalitions—is new. Industry has traditionally perceived environmental groups and legislators and regulators as adversarial. Some companies have intentionally avoided the media to minimize the potential for negative publicity; they have been reluctant to share information for fear of disclosing trade secrets. However, forward-thinking marketers are finding that fostering relationships with environmental stakeholders can reap big rewards. Constructive coalitions can help marketers:

- Anticipate problems and opportunities

- Obtain valuable input for initiatives and programs

- Foster dialogue that can result in greater objectivity

- Establish credibility with consumers and all constituents

- Enhance image and overall impact.

Consumers, environmental groups, government, the media, and retailers each have their own needs and agendas. This chapter details the challenges these different stakeholder groups pose to marketers and explores the specific opportunities afforded by building good relationships with them.

The Consumer as Stakeholder

Consumers are important stakeholders because purchasing behavior is based on their perceptions and their cooperation is vital to many of industry's environmental necessities such as reducing solid waste. Enlisting consumers' support provides marketers with the opportunity to maintain their loyalty and secure much needed cooperation. The challenge for marketers is to get consumers on their side by educating them on environmental issues and how to solve them.

Consumers' misperceive many environmental issues and this can result in lost opportunities for marketers, especially those who use plastic packaging.

Many consumers see packaging as unnecessary and wasteful. Packaging accounts for a third of landfill volume, yet consumers perceive it as much higher and a nationwide backlash against packaging is underway. Nearly 80% of consumers believe too much packaging is used. Half say they will reject products that appear overpackaged.

Consumers have especially distorted views about plastic. They perceive that plastic packaging represents up to 69% of packaging waste, while it actually accounts for only 13% by volume (See Exhibit 4.1.). The little understood reality is that paper and glass make up the bulk of packaging-related materials, yet in consumers' minds together they account for only 13%.

Compounding the issue, consumers do not understand the role packaging plays in the overall marketing process, or why specific packaging materials are chosen over others. The presence of some packaging materials, such as outercartons required for safe product transport and impactful in-store display, is perceived by many consumers as excessive and wasteful.

With solid waste problems predicted to become more acute, packaging will increasingly be scrutinized. In the future, what is perceived as excess packaging could well become a significant negative brand attrib-

EXHIBIT 4.1
Consumer Perceptions of Plastic in the Solid Waste Stream

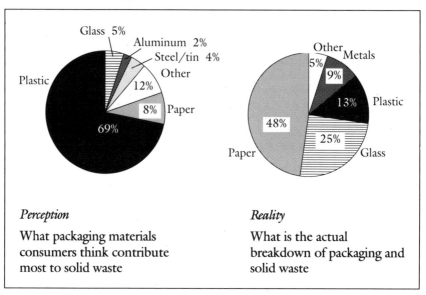

Perception

What packaging materials consumers think contribute most to solid waste

Reality

What is the actual breakdown of packaging and solid waste

Source: Franklin Associates, Gerstman & Meyers, (adjusted for 1991) as cited in *Food & Beverage Marketing*, Sept. 1990, p.34.

ute and cast an unfavorable halo on its manufacturer. Smart marketers will incorporate consumers' perceptions into package design and educate consumers on packaging's many benefits.

Representing another issue for marketers, many consumers perceive recycling as a complete answer to waste management problems. Research shows that consumers are much more likely to engage in recycling-related behaviors such as buying products that can be recycled, than behavior aimed at source reduction such as using refillable containers, and buying fewer disposables.

From a legislative standpoint, the implications of consumers' reliance on recycling can be significant: as of 1991, upwards of 60% of consumers

EXHIBIT 4.2
What Consumers Are Currently Doing
About Solid Waste Management

	1989 Total (292) %	1990 Total (313) %	1991 Total (318) %
Doing something	61	78	85
Recycling	54	70	78
Buy in recyclable containers	22	36	36
Buy in recycled containers	9	19	23
Use paper bags instead of plastic bags	11	24	22
Buy in biodegradable containers	9	18	18
Crush large items to take up less space	4	11	13
Buy in large sizes	1	7	7
Buy products with less/minimal packaging	2	10	11
Composting	4	9	12
Use refillable containers	—	9	10
Use fewer disposable items	—	17	13
Buy fewer products in individual portion sizes	NA	NA	
Not doing anything	39	22	15

*Less than 0.5%

Source: Consumer Solid Waste: Awareness, Attitude and Behavior Study III, Gerstman and Meyers, July, 1991.

were calling for packages to be recyclable or made from recycled content.[1] With landfills closing at a rapid rate and a limit on the amount of recyclable waste estimated at 25–50%, significant consumer attention will need to be focused on complementary solid waste management options such as source reduction, incineration and composting—as well as on recycling—in the years ahead.

NEED FOR EDUCATION

Clearly, we need a more informed public which is better equipped to make rational purchasing and policy decisions about products, packaging, and manufacturing processes. Industry has the relevant facts and technical information—not to mention the necessary regulatory and consumer incentives—to help clarify the issues. Indeed, several major marketers and trade groups are already undertaking major initiatives to influence the attitude and behavioral changes necessary to support waste reduction, recycling, composting, and incineration programs and garner support for environmentally sound products and processes. Many of these initiatives have the added benefit of engendering loyalty to the companies that take action while gaining public support for industry in general.

Among many advertising efforts that have been conducted, Dow Chemical has aired commercials showing how plastics can be recycled just like glass or aluminum. One spot, for example, showed a nature guide explaining how used plastic bottles can be converted into items such as the fiberfill for a hiker's vest. Similarly, print ads from Huntsman Chemical demonstrate how used polystyrene can find new life as playground equipment. Huntsman's vice president of corporate communications explains, "We want them to know that polystyrene is recyclable and is being recycled, and that Huntsman Chemical Company is truly active in recycling and other environmental issues."[2]

The Aseptic Packaging Council, an industry trade group, is aggressively educating consumers about the potential recyclability and source reduction benefits of its multi-layered juice boxes. The Council is now working with the state of Massachusetts to set up pilot recycling programs.

Ideas for Action

Use the following questions to help assess areas requiring consumers' support.

• How knowledgeable are our consumers on the environmental issues that affect our industry, company, and products?

• What types of messages do we need to be getting to consumers about the issues so as to improve our positioning long term?

• What do consumers need to know in order to use, recycle, and safely dispose of our products and packaging?

Children as Stakeholders

If adults represent an opportunity for marketers, addressing children's environmental concerns holds even more promise. Children not only represent a large buying force in and of themselves, but they increasingly influence their parents' purchasing decisions. As future consumers, they are stakeholders worth developing relationships with now.

Children learn about environmental issues in school and their deep, spirited concerns give them a strong incentive to get involved. They represent a powerful grassroots force for social change.

To students the environment represents a top social issue and they are becoming a well organized group. Teenagers were active boycotters of Star-Kist tuna and McDonald's restaurants. In announcing his company's shift to dolphin-free tuna, Heinz CEO, Anthony J. F. O'Reilly, read a handful of postcards he personally received from high school students with messages like, "How can you sleep at night knowing your company is doing this?"[3] In the Fall of 1990, members of Kids Against Pollution (KAP) sent 3,000 letters to McDonald's headquarters in Oak Brook, Illinois, demanding that the company eliminate its foam containers.

Ecology-savvy children are pestering parents to recycle and buy green products. More than one in three parents have changed their shopping behavior because of what they learned about the environment from their

children. Seventeen percent of all households with children have avoided
a product they ordinarily would have purchased because of influence
from a child, and 20% of parents report having purchased a product spe-
cifically because their children told them it was better for the environment.[4] With children influencing $28.3 billion in family grocery shop-
ping budgets, the opportunity they represent for marketers is huge.

College students are also on top of the environmental bandwagon. A
poll conducted in 1989 by UCLA's Higher Education Institute found
that 26% of college freshmen in the United States listed involvement in
programs to clean up the environment as a "very important" life goal.
Environmental courses are increasingly being given and some schools
now offer degree programs on the subject.

Like their younger brothers and sisters, many college students have
formed grassroots organizations such as Student Environmental Action
Coalition (SEAC) with 1,500 chapters on college and high school campuses.

According to *The New York Times*, in October 1990, SEAC organized
the largest environmental student meeting in history. Its subject was
corporate accountability. Over 8,000 students left the meeting seeking
boardroom reforms and vowing to boycott corporations in the process.
Coalition members at the University of Colorado boycotted Coors
beer, demanding less pollution in the Rocky Mountains. Students at the
University of New Mexico in Albuquerque boycotted acid- and stone-
washed jeans, which are made with pumice, a volcanic rock produced by
strip mining. Levi Strauss, the largest manufacturer of jeans, was the
principal target.

NEED TO EDUCATE CHILDREN

The next generation of environmentally aware consumers and citizens is
now in the offing. By the year 2000, today's 10-, 11-, and 12-year-olds
will be 18 or older and will be making their pro-environment sentiments
felt in workplaces, voting booths, and supermarkets. Given their influence on adults and their future buying power, just like their parents,
young children, teens, and college students need to be educated about
environmental issues and their roles in solid waste management.

Major marketers are already cultivating children's support and are reaping the benefits. Some provide tools and grants to educators, cooperate with national or local youth groups, and sponsor environmental projects like recycling or community cleanup events. They are reaching youth through environmental programming such as the Discovery Channel, Network Earth, and CNN's "Captain Planet" and through environmental clubs or environmental pictures, games, and puzzles inserted in product packages.

Extending their efforts to the younger set, Dow Chemical, among others, has launched a major program designed to educate teens about recycling efforts. Representing dramatically new communications strategies for a conservative company, Dow's program employs a live rock band and uses other techniques that can speak to teens in their own language. Entitled "Recycle This," the program has already helped 250,000 teens in more than 100 cities realize that to reduce the pressure on landfills, we all must practice the 3Rs—Reduce, Reuse, and Recycle. Research shows a dramatic rise in awareness of recycling issues, particularly relating to plastics.[5]

Educators are willing partners. Teachers welcome educational materials to help answer students' environmental questions. Recognizing the opportunity, McDonald's has distributed a 16-page educational magazine called *Wecology*, developed in conjunction with World Wildlife Fund and distributed to 5 million children around the nation through educator magazines, McDonald's restaurants, and schools. The magazine includes detailed feature stories on specific environmental issues such as global warming, and provides environmental tips. Celebrities like Cyndi Lauper and Alf, the TV character, are quoted.[6]

In 1991, with cooperation from the National Science Teachers Association, The Keyes Fibre Company, manufacturers of Chinet molded paper plates, launched the "Chinet Environmental Experiment" consisting of an in-classroom educational kit for grammar school students. Its purpose was to educate children about solid waste, the biodegradability of paper, and the long term viability of composting. Judy Meyenhofer, account executive at Myers Communicounsel who developed the kit, summarizes the opportunity that exists in engaging children's environmental support: "Habits are decided early in life. If you teach a kid at an early age what some of the answers are, they will make better decisions later."[7]

Ideas for Action

Ask the following questions to assess opportunities to enlist the support of children in your environmental activities.

- What role do children play in influencing the purchase of our products?

- How can we enlist children's support for our products and industry now?

- What opportunities exist to develop environmental education programs or curricula?

Government Stakeholders

Long viewed as an adversary to business, many marketers are finding that working with government can help to create balanced legislation. It can also pay off in access to technical resources and information that can provide competitive leverage and open the door to new marketing opportunities. A pro-active stance is required to take advantage of these opportunities.

An emotionally charged political issue that was largely ignored by the Reagan administration, the environment is now viewed by many office-holders as an issue with no political downside. In fact, ignoring the environment is no longer an option for elected officials desirous of pleasing an environment-anxious electorate.

As the major source of pollution, the pressure is on industry to clean up—a notion that sits well with consumers eager to maintain their lifestyles. Like their counterparts in Europe, voters are calling for stringent new laws built around the themes of "polluter pays" and "the producer should bear responsibility for recycling and waste disposal." With a government highly reactive to their demands, they are meeting with much success, though not all of it is beneficial to industry or the environment.

Of particular significance to industry, legislators and regulators don't always possess the necessary scientific expertise or knowledge of business processes. Consequently, legislation can often be misguided or unbalanced. Often it can result in unnecessary costs to industry that will ultimately need to be borne by consumers.

For example, spurred on by consumers, many state governments are pressing ahead on recycling at the expense of other options. Legislation has been passed or is pending in many states banning or taxing certain forms of packaging that promote source reduction, such as "brick packs" for coffee and aseptic packages (juice boxes) because they are not broadly recyclable like steel or aluminum cans and glass. Aseptic packaging, for example, has been banned from landfills in Maine since September 1990.

NEED TO BE PRO-ACTIVE

With environmental ills projected to get worse before they get better, expect the legislative machine to continue to churn. By participating in the development of new laws and rules rather than simply reacting to them, marketers can help to achieve environmental legislation that is workable and affordable. Forming coalitions with legislators and regulators aimed at sharing information and resources can help clarify the issues and obtain support for industry's dilemma as well as its initiatives.

The fragrance industry's management of proposed clean air legislation in California and ARCO's introduction of reformulated gasoline provide two relevant cases.

Fragrance Manufacturers Help Bring About Balanced Regulations

In 1991, to implement California's Clean Air Act, the California Air Resources Board (CARB), the agency responsible for implementing and enforcing clean air standards in the state, proposed a regulation that would require significant reformulation of all "personal fragrance products," an action that could have eliminated most popular perfumes, colognes, and aftershaves from the market. The goal was to reduce alcohol in these products.

Fragrance manufacturers, working through the Cosmetic, Toiletry, and Fragrance Association (CTFA), spent almost a year educating the CARB staff on why fragrances are dependent on alcohol as a solvent, and why it was impossible to reformulate existing products. The experience was a positive one. In January 1992, existing fragrance products were exempted from the regulations, and realistic standards and time limits for future products were set. According to Tom Donegan, vice president and general counsel of CTFA, "This experience underlined an important operating rule for industry. It is important to ensure early in the process that government officials understand your products, your industry, and the realistic consequences of their proposed actions.

"Initial proposals are not necessarily reflective of ill-will toward industry, but may be a product of ignorance or may be a trial balloon to get you to the bargaining table." Donegan continues, "After all, regulators don't want to upset consumers either; they are part of their constituency. If you make a convincing argument that consumers will be upset at the unnecessary loss of a popular product, regulators may be open to changing their proposals."[8]

Coalition Building Helped ARCO Clear the Way for Reformulated Gasoline

In March 1989, the South Coast Air Quality Management District (SCAQMD), the agency responsible for controlling air pollution in southern California, was crafting a long-range air pollution control plan. With the goal of reducing air pollution by 90% over the next 20 years, the agency's plan focused on gasoline which contributes nearly 60% of the air pollution in Southern California. The plan called for the complete phaseout of gasoline in favor of cleaner fuels like natural gas and ethanol.

Recognizing that one of its major markets would be cut off entirely, ARCO, the leading gasoline marketer in the West Coast, went to the SCAQMD with a proposed solution: they would develop reformulated gasoline. The proposal was then submitted to the regulators for close scrutiny. Using a computer model that had been developed by the

SCAQMD in conjunction with California Institute of Technology, ARCO researchers showed the SCAQMD that the reformulated gasoline could significantly reduce emissions in keeping with the standards being proposed by the SCAQMD.

As a result of this public/private initiative, ARCO's reformulated gasoline was approved for use in southern California. It was also written into the federal Clean Air Act amendments of 1990. As will be discussed in Chapter 6, the reformulated gasoline was introduced to consumers as Emission Control–1 (EC–1) gasoline with the full blessing of the SCAQMD.

Two years after the launch of EC–1, reformulated gasoline is the adopted fuel of the future for the state of California: the SCAQMD is now using an even cleaner version of EC–1 as the reference point for its gasoline standards, giving ARCO a distinct advantage over its competitors, who will be hard pressed to meet the same standard.[9]

There are important lessons to be learned from ARCO's experiences:

• Working with the local regulatory board opened the door to invaluable technical support to which ARCO did not otherwise have access.

• By working with SCAQMD, ARCO helped define the very rules by which it—and competitors—will be regulated.

Ideas for Action

Ask the following questions to assess opportunities for enlisting the support of government.

• What legislation is in effect or underway on the federal, state, and local levels that will affect our brands and company?

• What steps can we take to promote self-regulation and avoid mandatory regulations?

• How can we work to modify excessively restrictive legislation?

• Are there opportunities to pre-empt legislation to gain competitive advantage and demonstrate leadership?

Environmental Group Stakeholders

Many environmentalists and other advocacy groups whose agenda have often conflicted with those of industry are now allies of companies perceived as making significant environmental progress. Several companies, some of them major polluters, are finding much opportunity in building coalitions with these groups. Alliances with environmentalists can help marketers enhance impact, establish credibility with consumers and media, obtain valuable inputs for business and marketing planning, and, most importantly, ensure that a balanced point of view is communicated to all other stakeholders.

Environmental groups are key players in the environmental consumerism movement. With more than 16 million members worldwide, these groups are capable of making a mainstream impact far beyond the rainbow warriors of the 1970s and 1980s.

Environmentalists are no longer the college kids mimeographing flyers about the latest boycott; in the last 20 years, they have matured into sophisticated watchdogs and communicators. They are now organized into several powerful national organizations and more than 7,000 local groups, and they are highly adept at leveraging the mass media to enlist support for their cause. Some of the larger and more powerful groups such as the Sierra Club, the Natural Resources Defense Council (NRDC), and the Environmental Defense Fund (EDF) are staffed with premier lawyers and scientists. These professional environmentalists have become proficient at using pressure in Washington to counterbalance industrial lobbying and forge their own agendas.

The public supports their efforts. Not only do environmental groups enjoy the highest levels of credibility among consumers (see Chapter 3), but a 1990 *New York Times* poll found that a majority (60%) consider environmentalists to be "reasonable" people, while less than a third (27%) perceive them as extremist. As detailed in Exhibit 4.3, the number of consumers who support environmental groups has nearly tripled

EXHIBIT 4.3
Support of Environmental Groups

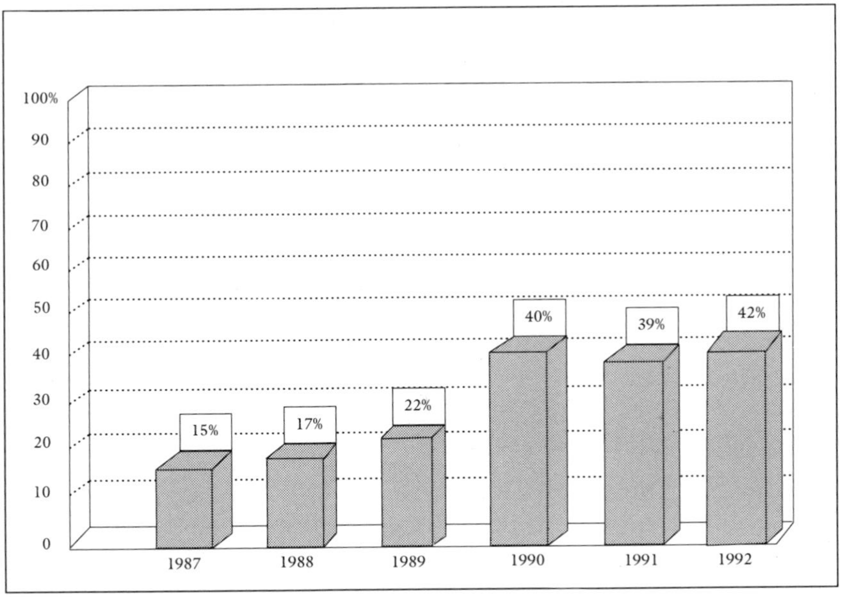

Source: Cambridge Reports/Research International 1992.

in 6 years. In addition, 16% of adults are currently members of an environmental group or have been within the past year. Twenty percent say they have volunteered for these groups during the past few years.[10]

Sophisticated tools, including advertising, are now part of an arsenal that is increasingly aimed at corporate America's bottom line. The environmentalists know that major companies and popular brands of consumer products make effective targets, and they are increasingly taking their cases *directly* to the people, utilizing effective media campaigns and boycotting companies that pollute. Of course, some might argue that their targets are misdirected, but the fact is that their efforts are highly effective. Consider the case of dolphin-safe tuna fishing practices. In 1990 dramatic ads sporting headlines like, "Kill a dolphin today. All you need is a tuna can and a can opener," were used to rally consumer support for a national boycott campaign against tuna canners that trapped dolphin in their nets. The efforts prompted legislation such as

The Dolphin Protection Consumer Information Act. The resulting public outcry and the threat of legislation forced Star-Kist and other major tuna marketers to switch to "dolphin-free" fishing methods. Pundits had predicted tremendous resistance to this costly change, but the threatened boycott brought about a bloodless coup.

Packaging has been singled out by environmentalists as particularly detestable. They are making packaging a primary symbol of America's convenience-driven society and a major contributor to garbage pile-ups.

For example, in 1989, the New York Public Interest Research Group (NYPIRG) released a consumer-directed booklet entitled *Plagued by Packaging*, which targeted major supermarket brands including Colgate-Palmolive's "Fab One Shot" laundry product and Kodak's "Fling" disposable camera. Colgate-Palmolive has since slimmed down its Fab package, and Kodak has instituted a recycling program for its cameras, now rechristened "Fun Saver."

Representing another grassroots effort, the Seattle-based Washington Citizens for Recycling (WCR) releases annual Packaging Booby Prizes from an Environmental Point of View. Packages that have been awarded booby prizes include toothpaste pumps, blister packs, and aseptic juice boxes.

All environmental group initiatives are not hostile to industry, however. Like consumers, environmentalists also come in many shades. Some extremist groups like Greenpeace, the original rainbow warriors, and Earthfirst!, which uses controversial tactics like spiking trees in its fight to save the spotted owl, refuse to dialogue with industry. Other, more moderate groups are finding that working with industry helps to achieve mutual objectives. Many groups support the development of more environmentally sound consumer products and are willing to help marketers in their efforts. Some even recommend specific brands to consumers that they perceive to be environmentally preferable. For example, in addition to its criticisms, WCR also gave awards to packaging they considered to be environmentally sound such as cardboard egg cartons, paper sugar sacks, and paper sleeve lightbulb packages. The Pennsylvania Resources Council publishes the *Environmental Shopping Guide* that lists brands such as Arm & Hammer baking soda and the Budget Gourmet line of frozen entrees. These products are lauded for their natural ingredients and more resource-efficient packaging. The Council on Economic Priorities bestows its coveted Corporate Conscience Award at an annual event that attracts CEOs from some of the biggest companies in America.

Marketers who develop constructive relationships with environmentalists now can expect long-term rewards. Environmental groups will continue to play a leading role in publicizing environmental problems and creating awareness of the links between environmental ills and industry. They will continue to mature as communicators; indeed with an increased social consciousness in the mainstream, environmental groups may find it increasingly easy to recruit professionals from the advertising and public relations communities, thereby strengthening their efforts. The alliances that are now being formed between environmental groups and manufacturers will only enhance environmentalists' credibility and sophistication.

OPPORTUNITIES TO DEVELOP ALLIANCES WITH ENVIRONMENTAL GROUPS

Environmental groups are aware of or are involved in the development of cutting edge ideas and technology that can help industry stay in the forefront of change. Getting their input can add credibility and impact to one's efforts. Because they are influential with the media, it behooves marketers to get their approval on claims before releasing them to the public.

As pointed out in *Green MarketAlert*, marketers can develop relationships with environmentalists by forming industry environmental group alliances designed to obtain support and guidance, by joining joint industry/advocacy group roundtables, and through cause-related marketing campaigns.

Industry/Environmental Group Alliances

Seek out consultants such as the joint task force that was developed in 1990 by McDonald's and the Environmental Defense Fund (EDF).

EDF staffers worked with McDonald's technical people to develop a 42-step action plan for reducing solid waste. The company won kudos from environmentalists, consumers, and the media for the breadth of the plan and for its willingness to claim a leadership role in waste reduction among the corporate community. The relationship helped the EDF project a leadership image and attract support for its organization.

In a similar vein, before announcing his "Dolphin Safe" Star-Kist policy to the Heinz Board of Directors and the public, CEO Anthony O'Reilly consulted with David Phillips, executive director of the Earth Island Institute, the environmental group which had been spearheading the nationwide boycott of tuna canners. Phillips set high standards for Heinz to meet, including a ban on dolphin-unsafe tuna throughout Heinz' operations worldwide; records of Heinz's compliance had to be open to inspection by Earth Island Institute, and Heinz had to support the Dolphin Protection Consumer Information Act. These agreements helped to win Heinz the respect of the environmental community, and by having a comprehensive policy that was acceptable to environmentalists, Heinz established itself as a leader among large corporations on environmental responsibility. And with Star-Kist's market share rising to a record 40% after the announcement, the enhanced reputation appeared to have helped the company's bottom line.

Industry/Advocacy Group Roundtables

Share information with environmentalists so as to better understand each other's points of view and help bring about workable solutions. The National Wildlife Federation (NWF), one of the largest environmental groups in the United States, has established a formal roundtable called the Corporate Conservation Council. It provides a forum where corporate executives can engage in frank and open discussions with NWF leadership about emerging environmental and natural resource issues. Environmentalists and leaders from major corporations including AT&T, 3M, and Johnson & Johnson exchange ideas and explore proposals for improving environmental quality. Environmentalists discover what obstacles exist among industry to achieving their agendas, while business leaders learn what types of initiatives environmentalists will support.

One executive describes the value of engaging in this type of information exchange this way: "Environmentalists affect legislation. By engaging in closed-door sessions, a businessperson gets to understand the environmentalists' philosophy. Environmentalists are my consumers, too. Just like with regular consumers, you need to understand their attitudes. I consider these sessions to be like focus groups with consumers. I learn where their heads are at on these types of issues."

Cause-Related Sponsorships

Enlist environmentalists' direct efforts for marketing programs. With cause-related marketing, everybody wins: consumers can contribute to favorite environmental programs, industry enjoys added credibility and impact for its efforts, and environmentalists receive broadscale publicity with the potential of adding new members and attracting financial support. *Special Events Reports* projects that cause-related sponsorships will represent 8% of total marketing sponsorships, or $262 million in 1992, up from 7% or $231 million in 1991.[11]

S.C. Johnson Wax has embraced cause-related marketing. In 1990 and 1991, S.C. Johnson cooperated with the World Wildlife Fund (WWF) in a program that allowed consumers to make contributions to the We Care for America grant fund administered by WWF. The fund supports a number of research projects to help promote clean air, clean water, and clean earth. Consumers specified one of these three environmental research areas to which a 10-cent donation was made when a coupon, delivered to over 40,000,000 households was redeemed. Retailers also participated by adding research area designations of their own, to which a percentage of consumers' purchases was donated.

To date, the We Care for America coupon program raised $1 million, thereby making possible 23 different new environmental technology projects. According to Jane Hutterly, director, environmental affairs worldwide for S. C. Johnson Wax, a major strength of the program was its reach into more than 90% of American households with the message that individual actions can make a difference. Having WWF as a partner brought the program and S.C. Johnson Wax credibility and impact.

> **Ideas for Action**
> Ask the following questions to assess opportunities for enlisting the support of environmental groups.
>
> • How are our company, our products, and our packaging viewed by environmentalists?
>
> • Is factual information on our products, company, and category being disseminated by environmentalists?
>
> • Can environmental groups provide us with needed expertise?
>
> • Can we educate environmentalists on the positive aspects of our products and processes?
>
> • Are our environmental initiatives worthy of receiving special environmental group recognition?
>
> • Are there opportunities to enhance perceptions of our company's and brands' images by sponsoring a joint promotion with an environmental group?

Media Stakeholders

Quick to broadcast environment-related accidents and to point out ways that popular products can harm the environment, media can also be responsive to industry's pro-active initiatives. A cooperative spirit is critical to developing this opportunity, and education will be needed to make sure that messages conveyed to consumers are accurate and fair.

Environmental disasters are media-friendly. Blazing rainforests, slaughtered elephants, oil-slicked otters, and medical waste rolling up on once pristine beaches all make good news stories. Since the Fall of 1987, when the Mobro garbage barge sailed from Islip, Long Island in search of a dumpsite, virtually every consumer and news magazine, including *Life, Newsweek, Time,* and *National Geographic* have run cover stories on the environment.

The media are treating environmental issues seriously, ensuring top-of-mind consumer awareness of the issues. Radio and television stations are assigning top-flight reporters to the environmental beat, and TV news broadcasts are covering the issues much more extensively than ever before. According to *Channels* magazine the number of network news minutes devoted to coverage of environment issues jumped 76% from 1988 to 1989. No other category increased nearly as much.

Hollywood celebrities like Robert Redford, Barbra Streisand, and Meryl Streep are creating broadscale awareness for environmental issues and making it fashionable to be an environmentalist. Two organizations in Hollywood, Earth Communications Office and Environmental Media Associates, have sprung up to promote pro-environmental themes in regular TV programming and the movies, and a specialty environmental consumer press, now in its infancy, is picking up steam. Magazines such as *Garbage, Buzzworm, E,* and *Trilogy* target those concerned about the environment, the thought leaders who are likely to influence everyone else. Influentials also read the slick publications such as *Sierra, Audubon,* and *World Watch* offered by environmental groups. Books on the environment top bestseller lists—*50 Simple Things You Can Do To Save the Earth* has sold more than 1.8 million copies.

Most consumers get the bulk of their information on environmental matters from the media, and particularly television. Of issue to marketers, media is a far more credible source of information than industry. However, while powerful in its scope and impact, the media can fall short of getting consumers all the facts they need to make balanced decisions. Many reporters are not expert on environmental topics. Information tends to be delivered in sound bytes that are seldom capable of lending a balanced perspective to the issues. With competition for viewers so intense, stories are often skewed to the dramatic. All too often, industry ends up being pitted against the environment. The consequences of all this can be devastating. Recall that media attention to the link between rainforest depletion and cattle grazing resulted in consumer pressure on restaurants to use only domestically grown beef. And it was media coverage that sparked a nationwide consumer scare against the Alar pesticide in 1988 that cost applegrowers an estimated $100 million in sales.

With environmental ills projected to get worse before they get better, expect media to continue to galvanize environmentally aware consumers. Clearly there is an immediate need and opportunity for industry to pro-actively engage the media while attitudes are still forming. However, in order to enlist the media's support, marketers will need to overcome two barriers: an uncooperative reputation and lack of credibility.

When asked to name their greatest frustration in dealing with business people, journalists in a national survey cited most frequently "inaccessibility," "insensitivity to deadlines," "no comment," and "excessive technical jargon."[12] No wonder that, in the same survey, only 29 of 100 business leaders agreed that the news media has done a good job of "balancing the concerns of business/industry with those of environmentalists."

A qualitative poll conducted by *TJFR Business News Reporter* of 50 leading environmental journalists in late 1991 revealed a credibility gap between the media and corporations on environmental issues. The poll found that given a choice of putting their trust in environmental groups, government officials, scientists, other news organizations, or business executives, environmental reporters overwhelmingly ranked corporate America last. The survey also found that fewer than half of the journalists questioned said they rely even periodically upon interviews with corporate executives as sources for their reports. (See Exhibit 4.4.)

HOW TO WORK WITH MEDIA

Marketers can enlist the support of media by providing technical support to reporters, pro-actively educating the media on corporate and product initiatives, and sponsoring media events that directly address local environmental issues.

Procter & Gamble is just one company that recognizes the importance of being accessible to the media today. According to H.E. "Zeke" Swift, environmental marketing manager, "Communicating with the media is consistent with our policy of informing consumers, employees, community groups, and other constituencies about the environmental quality of our company's products and packaging."[13] Smaller companies, like The Body Shop, have been able to leverage so much press attention that they do not need to advertise. Other companies, such as First Brands Corporation, have succeeded in developing powerful grassroots

EXHIBIT 4.4
Environmental Journalists' Trusted Sources

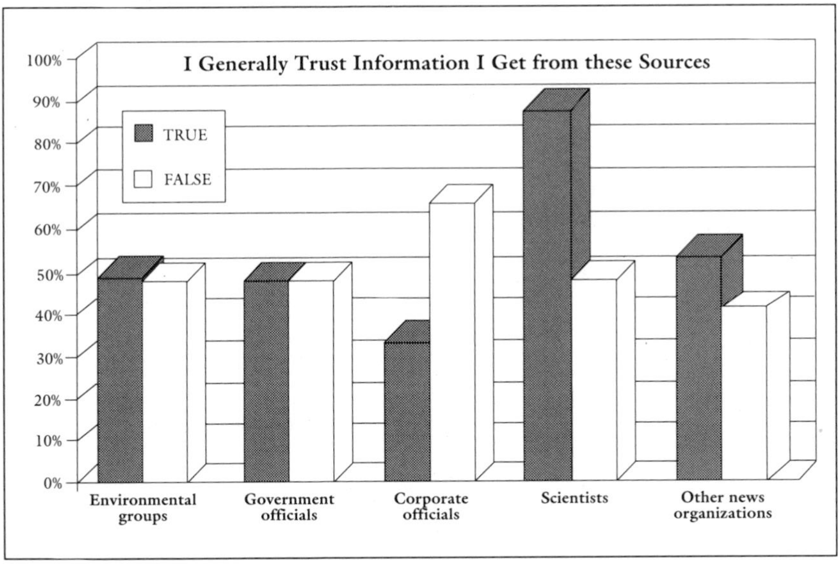

Source: *TJFR Business News Reporter*, Jan. 1992. Reprinted with permission.

environmental media efforts capable of capturing media attention and goodwill.

GLAD Bag-A-Thon Captures Attention of Local Media

Since 1986, First Brands Corporation, the makers of GLAD trash bags, has conducted an annual GLAD Bag-A-Thon event with the nonprofit organization Keep America Beautiful (KAB). From one five-city pilot program, the effort has grown to become the country 's largest organized cleanup and recycling effort. Coordinated through local mayors' offices and KAB affiliates, and supported by retailers, it now involves more than 725,000 volunteers in more than 100 cities and towns, and collects approximately 18 million pounds of recyclables and litter per year.

One of the program's outstanding features is that it allows communities to select their own project, whether it be turning a vacant lot into a park or picking up litter in a designated area of town.

In addition to better community relations and extra business, the Bag-A-Thon has resulted in strong publicity and solid local relationships with the media. In 1991, for example, more than 2,000 media stories and 142 hours of public service announcements were broadcasted to rally support for the event.

Like Mobil's Hefty trash bags, GLAD bags were involved in the controversy over degradable plastics. However, Mobil took much of the public rebuke. One reason why First Brands and their GLAD bags largely stayed out of the argument may be the brand's long history of community service as well as the positive media relations built up over time as a result of the GLAD Bag-A-Thon program.

Ideas for Action

Ask some of the following questions to assess the strengths of your relationship with the media and discover opportunities for enlisting their support.

- How does the media view our company, brands, and industry?

- Are our company and brand getting coverage for our environmental initiatives?

- How are we handling questions and requests for information from the media?

- Which reporters cover our industry? What is their relationship with our company? Are they well-versed on the issues? Do they cover the issues in a well-balanced manner?

- Are any of our initiatives newsworthy or topical?

- Do we need to educate the media on technical issues?

- Can we take advantage of opportunities to support environmental authors?

Retailer Stakeholders

Retailers are on the front line of consumer concern, and they have their own environmental issues to manage, particularly regarding solid waste. At the same time, they have direct access to affluent green consumers—and know it. Marketers who build coalitions with retailers aimed at solving their needs and the needs of their customers will enjoy enhanced sales and strengthened vendor relationships.

Acknowledging the spending power of upscale consumers who are looking for green products, and desirous of preempting legislation that would require them to take back unwanted packaging, many retailers are assuming a proactive stance. They are demanding more environmentally responsible products and packaging from vendors. Some have gone so far as to create their own green brands.

To take advantage of opportunities to gain their customers' loyalty, many retailers are initiating on-site recycling programs. About half of the country's 31,000 grocery stores now recycle plastic bags.[14] A small but growing number of retailers are looking to protect their own credibility by hiring independent testing organizations to screen the environmental claims made by manufacturers.

Health food stores now carry a wide array of green products, and hundreds of specialty stores have sprung up around the country to serve the needs of deep green consumers. Increasingly, however, major retailers are stocking greener products and inaugurating special green sections in their stores. This represents a major opportunity to manufacturers of nationally distributed brands.

Sears, Roebuck & Co.

Sears has asked its 2,300 vendors to become environmental partners in reducing excess packaging by 25% by 1995. Four quotas were given to suppliers: reduce packaging volume and weight by at least 10% by 1994, increase the level of recycled materials in corrugated containers to 20% by 1996, increase the use of recycled materials in plastic containers by 1996, and utilize the highest recycled content materials in other types of packaging such as folded cartons and blister cards. The quotas will help save an estimated $5 million annually.

Wal-Mart

An early innovator of environmental marketing, Wal-Mart launched an in-store merchandising program in 1989, in which environmentally preferable products and packaging were rewarded with special shelf-talkers. Currently the chain has aggressive parking lot recycling and consumer education programs. Representing a major source of future opportunities for marketers, Wal-Mart plans to open a prototype green store in Spring 1993 that will feature environmentally sound products and comprehensive on-site recycling efforts.

Paul Higham, vice president of marketing for Wal-Mart, explains how the chain's many environmental initiatives are spurred by consumers:

> Whenever you have a movement of any sort in this country, it begins with idealists who tend toward an extremely polarized view. But this is an issue that started because of real problems and concerns people had in their own neighborhoods, such as insufficient landfill capacity and questions regarding the quality of the water we drink and the air we breathe. . . . The reality is that all of the idealistic statements that we have heard over recent years have now been translated into more pragmatic approaches such as sorting recyclables in the home and using municipal or private drop-offs. The average American knows infinitely more about these issues today than they did two years ago, and as people continue to learn more and more about what they can do, we see more and more people getting involved. At Wal-Mart we're seeing that sentiment expressed in more and more letters from our customers.[15]

The Home Depot

The Home Depot is just one major retailer that requires that manufacturers have their environmental claims reviewed by an independent organization. The 184-store chain also offers customers a "greenprint"— an environmental map of a house that points out where environmentally sound products and practices can be used and implemented. Mark Eisen, the chain's environmental manager, reports that "The greenprint has achieved its objectives of raising awareness among consumers for the environmental impact of the products they buy. It has received favorable comments from consumers, government, the press, and environmentalists."

TEAM UP WITH RETAILERS

Many marketers are finding that teaming up with retailers on behalf of the environment can produce added sales and in-store merchandising support, as well as strengthened vendor relationships. With major retail chains now developing more comprehensive environmental merchandising, recycling, and consumer educational programs, the potential to educate and convert that broad swath of passive green consumers is immense.

Marketers can leverage this opportunity by educating retailers on environmental issues and the specific environmental benefits of their products and packaging, helping retailers to set up recycling programs, and by developing green promotional programs.

In Germany, marketers and retailers are feverishly working to set up a national recycling program to forestall the implementation of legislation that would allow unwanted packaging to be returned to retailers, manufacturers, and ultimately to packaging manufacturers. The Dual System Deutschland has been formed to collect, sort, and recycle empty packaging throughout the country. Green Dot emblems will be displayed on recyclable packaging. German households will receive a special yellow garbage can with which to collect their Green Dot packaging.

Exide and Church & Dwight are just two of many manufacturers who are working with retailers here in the United States to manage environmental issues in ways that benefit all parties. Church & Dwight's program demonstrates the potential of enlisting several stakeholders in one orchestrated effort.

Exide and K mart Team Up to Recycle Lead Acid Batteries

There is considerable pressure now to keep the 2.5 billion batteries that are sold annually out of landfills. Batteries contain heavy metal and toxic chemicals that can leach out of landfills into groundwater. To help preempt legislation that would require retailers to set up their own collection programs and to take advantage of opportunities to re-use lead, in 1990 Exide joined forces with K mart to collect used automotive batteries. Consumers are given $1 for every used battery they bring back to stores.

The effort results in an all-win situation: 6.5 million lead acid batteries have been kept out of landfills, K mart is able to demonstrate environmental leadership among its customers, and Exide secures a cost effective source of lead for use in making future batteries.[16]

Enviro-centers Educate Consumers and Help Sell Baking Soda

In 1990, Church & Dwight launched highly successful Enviro-centers, special end-aisle displays that retailers stocked with alternative household cleaning products such as lemon juice, white vinegar, and Arm & Hammer baking soda. The Enviro-centers came packed with consumer educational materials developed in conjunction with Clean Water Fund, a 600,000-member national environmental organization dedicated to protecting water resources.

The Enviro-centers have paid off for Church & Dwight and the environmental community. This cooperative approach to environmental education ensured objective information was being disseminated to consumers. The benefit to the company was an enhanced corporate image and attendant sales increases. In 1991, for the first time in several years, Arm & Hammer baking soda showed a significant increase in sales volume. In the same year, Arm & Hammer laundry detergent became one of America's leading brands despite minimal advertising.[17]

Ideas for Action

Ask the following questions to assess opportunities to enlist the support of retailers.

• What are the most important environmental issues facing our key retailers in their trading areas?

• What types of education and training do buyers and sales personnel require about environmental issues for our brand/category?

• To what extent are our retailers aware of our environmental initiatives and the environmentally sound attributes of our products and packaging?

• What are the opportunities for our brand to get enhanced sales and in-store support from the most environmentally aware/concerned retailers?

1. Does our brand represent an environmental business opportunity to our retailers—to increase profits? Bring green consumers into the store?
2. How can we help to *solve* our retailer's environmental problems?
3. Can we provide retailers with technical support or educational materials for consumers?
4. Can we establish a joint recycling program for our products and/ or packaging?
5. Would subjecting our brands to independent certification enhance our distribution or our credibility?

Building coalitions with environmental stakeholders is a key strategy of effective environmental marketing. Coalition building can also provide marketers with vital support in addressing consumers' environmental concerns and prepare them for the next steps: developing greener products that consumers will like, communicating product and corporate initiatives with credibility and impact, and creating strategies for developing greener products. These are discussed in the next chapter.

Notes

1. "Consumer Solid Waste: Awareness, Attitude, and Behavior Study III," Gerstman & Meyers, Inc., July 1991.

2. Miller, Cyndee, "Use of Environment-Friendly Packaging May Take a While," *Marketing News*, Mar. 19, 1990, p.18.

3. Better, Nancy Marx, "Green Teens," *New York Times Magazine*, Mar. 8, 1992, p.66.

4. INFOCUS, Princeton, N.J., as reported in *Newark Star-Ledger*, Jan. 8, 1992, p.2.

5. Butcher, Michael, The Dow Chemical Company, presentation to Association of National Advertisers' Environmental Communications Forum, Mar. 12, 1992.

6. "The McNext Generation," *Restaurant Business*, Apr. 19, 1991, p.132.

7. Telephone conversation with J. Meyenhofer, Apr. 3, 1992.

8. Correspondence with Tom Donegan, June 6, 1992.

9. Kresser/Craig Case Study: ARCO Emission Control Guidelines, Kressor/Craig Advertising, Santa Monica, CA.

10. *Environment U.S.A.*, The Angus Reid Group, Toronto, Canada, 1991.

11. *Green MarketAlert*, Feb. 1992, p.12.

12. *1991 National Survey*, Knapp, Inc., Atlanta, as reported by *Green Marketing Report*, Jan. 1992, p.7.

13. Telephone conversation with H.E. Swift, Procter & Gamble, June 7, 1992.

14. *Green MarketAlert*, Jan. 1992, p.11.

15. Pellet, Jennifer, "It's Not Easy Being Green," *Discount Merchandiser*, Feb. 1992, p.70.

16. Telephone conversation with Joseph Calio, Exide, July 1992.

17. Correspondence with Bryan Thomlison, Church & Dwight, Feb. 1992.

Chapter 5

HOW TO DEVELOP GREENER PRODUCTS THAT CONSUMERS WILL LIKE—AND BUY

Developing environmentally sound products that consumers will buy is highly challenging, and the rewards are great. Green products are destined to replace ungreen products on the supermarket shelf. More and more marketers are finding that environment-related product strategies can enhance existing benefits, thus yielding products that last longer, taste better, and, in many instances, cost less—the stuff of which increased share, new sales opportunities, and enhanced imagery are made of. Marketers who reap the biggest product-related rewards will take the time now to research and execute strategies that offer the most significant benefits to the environment. Three guidelines can help:

1. Adopt a thorough approach to product greening. Assess the environmental implications of a product at every phase in its life cycle.

2. Take the high road—maximize potential return by focusing on cutting edge technologies. Opt for source reduction over recycling whenever possible.

3. Incorporate consumers' desires for high quality, affordability, and convenience, as discussed in Chapter 2.

Need for a Thorough Approach

Upgrading products and packaging to meet consumers' environmental expectations can be tricky. What may appear to be an environmental benefit may actually result in little or no value to the environment; manufacturers of degradable trash bags learned this lesson the hard way. Sometimes, the presumed "greening" of one attribute can actually heighten environmental impact. CPC, the makers of Mueller's pasta, found that converting to recycled carton material would actually add about 20% to the width of their packaging material. This would at least partially offset savings to the environment, considering the added energy needed to ship the new boxes.[1]

For these reasons, and also to prevent a backlash from consumers, environmental groups, regulators, and the media and other stakeholders, all of whom may be quick to point out the shortcomings of products and packaging, a thorough approach to "greening" is required. A tool called life cycle inventory (LCI) can help.

LCI is a process that quantifies the use of energy, resources, and emissions to the environment associated with a product throughout its life cycle. It accounts for the environmental impact of raw materials procurement, manufacturing and production, packaging, distribution, and in-use characteristics straight through to after-use and disposal.

An LCI of cotton versus disposable diapers, for example, would quantify the amount of pesticides and water used to grow cotton, as well as the water and energy needed for manufacture the diapers and transport them to stores and homes. Finally, it would consider the amount of water and energy used to launder the cloth diapers. An LCI of disposable diapers would take into account the environmental implications of cutting down and processing trees for wood pulp, along with the environmental burdens of extraction and refining of the petroleum required to produce the plastic backsheets. It would quantify the energy used in manufacturing and transportation, as well as how much solid waste was eventually sent to landfills. Exhibit 5.1 highlights the results of an LCI commissioned by Procter & Gamble comparing the relative environmental impacts of cloth versus paper disposable diapers.

Initially developed during the energy crisis of the 1970s to help reduce the amount of energy used for developing and distributing products, LCI is extremely useful for:

- Comparing energy and resource usage and environmental emissions associated with *existing products* and their alternatives

- Identifying significant *areas for improvement* in energy use and waste reduction

- Evaluating energy and resource usage and environmental emissions associated with *proposed changes* in manufacturing, or packaging of products.[2]

In the past 20 years, several organizations, including Franklin Associates (Prairie Village, KS), the Battelle Institute (Columbus, OH), Ar-

EXHIBIT 5.1
Environmental Burdens: Cloth versus Disposable Diapers

	Cloth	*Disposable*
Raw material consumption (lbs.)	3.6	25.3
Water consumption (gal.)	144	23.6
Energy consumption (BTUs)	78,890	23,290
Air emissions (lbs.)	0.860	0.093
Water polluton (lbs.)	0.117	0.012
Solid waste (lbs.)	0.24	22.18

Source: Arthur D. Little Co., as reprinted in *The New York Times*, July 14, 1990.

thur D. Little Co. (Cambridge, MA), Scientific Certification Systems (Oakland, California), and the Tellus Institute (Boston, Massachusetts), have performed life cycle inventories for companies in a broad range of industries including paper/paperboard, glass, steel, aluminum, and plastic beverage containers and delivery systems, building materials, transportation products, and others.

Caution is advised for using life cycle inventory as a marketing tool. Many life cycle inventories performed to date and leveraged for marketing purposes have been criticized for favoring the sponsor. For example, the LCI sponsored by Procter & Gamble comparing cloth versus disposable diapers concluded that when energy and water associated with collecting and washing the cloth diapers were accounted for, the total environmental impacts of the cloth were roughly equal to the disposables. This research conflicted with findings from an LCI commissioned by the National Association of Cloth Diaper Services which found cloth to be environmentally superior to paper disposables.[3] Two independent non-profit consumer product testing organizations—Green Seal and Scientific Certification Systems—are now working with experts in industry, government, and academia to legitimize the use of life cycle inventory and other cradle-to-grave approaches as marketing tools.

Monsanto is one company that is using LCI strategically. A. Frances Werner of Monsanto suggests that manufacturers "collect all easily available data about a product's life cycle, then prioritize and focus resources on fixing the problems that become apparent early in the analysis process. While improvements are being made, additional data can be accumulated."[4]

As presently developed, life cycle inventory focuses on the raw material requirements and waste and pollution emissions associated with producing a product. However, many environmental concerns are not addressed by LCI. According to Martin Wolf, a consultant on life cycle inventory and green product development, LCI must be augmented with a holistic evaluation of a product's environmental impact. Renewable or sustainable resource use, habitat destruction, biodiversity depletion, odors, visual pollution, noise pollution, toxicity, biodegradability, and other issues that are of concern to environmentalists and consumers cannot be evaluated by the quantitative approach of LCI and must be considered separately.

Green Product Development Issues

According to Wolf, holistically oriented environmental product issues can be grouped into four areas: raw materials acquisition and processing, manufacturing and distribution, product use and packaging, and after use and disposal. They incorporate a number of sub-issues, as detailed below.

Raw Materials Acquisition and Processing

- Conservation of natural resources like water, land, and air

- Protection of natural habitats and endangered species

- Waste minimization and pollution prevention, especially the use and release of toxics

- Transportation

- Use of renewable resources; sustainable use of resources

- Use of recycled materials

Manufacturing and Distribution Issues

- Minimal use of materials

- Toxics use/release

- Waste generation/handling

- Energy efficiency

- Water use

- Emissions to air, land, water

Product Use and Packaging Issues

- Energy efficiency

- Conservation of natural resources such as water required for the use of the product

- Consumer health and environmental safety

After-use/Disposal Issues

- Recyclability, and ease of reuse, remanufacture, and repair

- Durability

- Biodegradability

- Safe when incinerated or landfilled

Take the High Road

Maximize the long-term payout of product development efforts by adopting the most environmentally sound technology, materials, and design possible within the constraints of economics and consumer acceptance. This has many benefits. It can provide opportunities to preempt competition and costly legislation. In the process, it can often lead to positive publicity and enhanced brand and corporate imagery.

Also, try to solve the most significant long-term issue associated with your products and packaging. Most often, this will entail pursuing a source reduction strategy.

3M and Procter & Gamble demonstrate the potential of a high road product development strategy:

- 3M's Safest Stripper paint stripper is formulated with a water base instead of methylene chloride, a suspected carcinogen. It may ultimately boost 3M's market share. The Consumer Product Safety Commission announced in 1990 that all wood furniture strippers containing methylene chloride must now identify the chemical as a carcinogen.

With the consumer and regulatory climate as it is, methylene chloride may one day be banned or face surcharges that would favor water-based products.

Meanwhile, the low-fume, more pleasant-to-use formula has helped to expand the market for paint strippers by attracting first-timers to furniture stripping. Also, the product can be used indoors during the winter months and this has helped to extend product seasonality. The water-based formula also brings convenience benefits: no skin protection (such as rubber gloves) is required, and hands and tools can be cleaned with water rather than a chemical wash.

- Borrowing on a concept being utilized in Europe for its Lenor counterpart, Procter & Gamble's Downy fabric softener refill consists of a concentrated formula that is designed to be reconstituted with water poured back into the original plastic jug. This unique configuration yields a hefty (75%) packaging reduction versus its full-strength counterpart. The refill, which is also more profitable to make, accounts for 40% of Downy's total $258 million business. Strategically, the refill helps P&G to preempt legislation. In fact, laws have already been passed in California and Oregon requiring that by 1995 all rigid plastic packaging be either source-reduced, refillable, recyclable at a certain rate, or made from recycled content. With the outlook for plastics recycling uncertain, source reduction will help P&G meet these laws with ease. Meanwhile, other benefits accrue, not to mention a raft of corporate publicity for developing a revolutionary product and package that significantly reduces waste.

Strategies for Success

With the help of a little creativity, imagination, and, in some cases, new materials and/or technology, marketers all over the world are discovering myriad opportunities for products that please consumers and the environment. Using strategies as detailed below, many marketers are growing their businesses by addressing specific environmental issues that are most relevant to their consumers. In the process, they are saving money, enhancing corporate and brand imagery while ensuring future sales for their products. Listed below are just a few of the many products that are meeting consumers' emerging environmental needs while generating sales and profits for marketers. Note that some products are not new to the market; their inherent environmental benefits should help them enjoy renewed growth in the years ahead.

MINIMIZE DIRECT ENVIRONMENTAL IMPACT

While consumers are now focusing on product and packaging attributes—those features that they can see and feel—awareness is growing for how the environmental impact of various raw material procurement practices and manufacturing processes affects overall quality.

The makers of Earth's Best, an organically grown baby food, assert that organically grown food not only helps to minimize the environmental and health impacts of synthetic pesticide and fertilizer use, but it tastes better, too. That's why upscale restaurants on the East and West Coasts purchase organically grown foods whenever possible, and it's a key reason why Earth's Best's sales double every year. In only five years, Earth's Best has garnered 15% of the market for strained baby foods in some parts of the country despite stiff competition from Gerber, Beechnut, and Heinz. This growth is being spurred on by supermarket owners who believe that Earth's Best baby food offers the consumer a significant benefit as well as strong word of mouth endorsements from mothers who see the brand as an investment in good nutrition—the product is also made without added salt, sugar, or starch.

According to Jon Corcoran, director of communications for Earth's Best, the key to the brand's success comes down to quality. Says Corcoran, "We have a quality product that's in sync with changing priorities." He explains that consumers increasingly understand the importance of optimal infant health, and maintains that "diet is increasingly going to be seen as the first line of prevention; the food industry is fast becoming a health industry." Earth's Best is way out in front of this curve.[5]

Esprit's Ecollection line of clothing incorporates green manufacturing processes with the intent of minimizing environmental impact. Buttons are carved from nuts, handpainted wood, or reconstituted glass, and some of the cloth is organically grown or vegetable-dyed. Mechanically pre-shrinking knitted fabrics rather than using a chemical process eliminates resins and formaldehyde. Zippers are made from nonrusting alloys that are not electroplated. The full line of clothing, including pants, jackets, and shirts, is classicly styled to ensure maximum wear. The line is now moving into the company's 200 retail stores worldwide and into shops of deep green retailers such as Fred Segal in Santa Monica and Terra Verde in New York. Initial sales are "going very well."[6]

Melitta's Natural Brown coffee filters are another example of a product manufactured with the goal of minimizing environmental impact. They are not bleached with chlorine, thus helping to prevent dioxins and other toxic pollutants from being released into waterways. Some consumers perceive dioxin to be hazardous to health. Despite a 15% price premium in some markets, 1991 U.S. sales of Melitta's filters have increased 41% over 1990 and now account for 26% of Melitta's U.S. cone filter business. In Germany, unbleached coffee filters represent 60% of the total market.[7]

SOURCE REDUCE PRODUCTS AND PACKAGING

Many marketers are discovering that when it comes to source reduction, i.e., using less materials, less is more. Because source-reduced products and packages often cost less to produce, cost savings can be passed along to consumers. These products, which are often more convenient for the consumer, can also be more efficient for retailers to warehouse and stock. Following is a sampling of the many strategic opportunities to use source-reduced products and packaging.

Eliminate Packaging

Procter & Gamble has eliminated the outercartons on its Sure and Secret antiperspirants. This move, which required some adjustments to the primary package, has helped to eliminate 80 million outercartons per year, thereby reducing production costs by 20% and saving 3.4 million pounds of waste.[8]

Lightweight Packaging

Coca-Cola is just one of many companies that has lightweighted its packaging over the last several years, primarily as a cost savings measure. Aluminum cans have been lightweighted by 35%. Soft drink bottles made from polyethylene terephthalate (PET) plastic are now 21% lighter, and 16-ounce non-returnable glass bottles have been lightweighted by 23%.[9]

Similarly, versus five years ago, S.C. Johnson's steel aerosol cans use 35% less tin and at least 25% recycled steel content.[10] From an environmental standpoint, lightweighting not only saves natural resources and material costs but helps to cut down on energy use during transportation.

Concentrate Products

Superconcentrated powdered laundry detergents such as Lever Brothers' Wisk Power Scoop not only create less waste and are more energy efficient (lighter to ship), but they take up as little as one-quarter of the space on retailer shelves and are cheaper to transport and warehouse. Consumers like the fact that they are easier to carry and store. They are already commonplace in Japan and growing rapidly in Europe where space is at a premium; in the United States, the market share for all compact detergents represents half of the $2.1 billion powder segment, and is projected to represent the lion's share of all powders in the future.[11]

Use Bulk Packaging/Large Sizes

All-purpose cleaners such as Fantastik, 409, and Glass Plus have long come in large sizes for refilling. Bulk packs use less packaging per product and save consumers money.

Develop Multi-purpose Products

S.C. Johnson's Agree Shampoo Plus Conditioner represents just one of many multi-purpose products that combine two products into one. To boot, the product is now being tested in an "Enviro-pouch" which uses 80% less plastic than conventional bottles and weighs 85% less than a rigid plastic bottle. The pouch, which requires no closure, is collapsible so it reduces solid waste by 92% over uncrushed bottles. The stand-up Enviro-pouch is lightweight, self sealing, and strong, so it gives consumers an opportunity to choose environmentally responsible packaging without sacrificing quality or convenience.[12] Other multi-purpose products include detergent with bleach and all-purpose cleaners that can be used on a variety of surfaces.

USE RECYCLED CONTENT

Using recycled content in some manufacturing processes can help reduce toxics as well as save resources. Steel, aluminum, paper, and glass have historically been recycled as a cost savings measure. Thanks to advances in technology, as well as a little ingenuity, plastics are increasingly finding life as economical new materials as well.

Marcal Paper Company is saving money and adding value to its full line of economically-priced household paper products by using recycled phone books, undeliverable third class mail collected from regional post offices, and other waste papers in its production processes. The use of recycled papers not only helps extend the life of local landfills, but it provides a savings for local taxpayers: the 175 post offices from which Marcal collects used paper estimate that they will save the local communities over half a million dollars per year in trash hauling fees.[13] Marcal also benefits. Trucks that used to return from their routes empty will now use those same trips to haul materials back to the factory.

Corrugated cardboard has been collected for recycling by retailers, wholesalers, and distributors for years. Now Apple Computers is pioneering the use of recycled corrugated cardboard for direct-to-consumer shippers. Using an environmentally preferable two-pronged approach, Apple has switched from white (bleached) shipping cartons to brown (unbleached) cartons made from partially recycled content. Omar Khalifa, manager for design for the environment of Apple reports that the use of unbleached paperboard boxes with added recycled content will not only result in long-term cost savings to the company, but research with Apple customers indicated that the move provided a "reaffirmation of what Apple is and what it stands for."[14]

Thirty percent of PET soft drink bottles are currently being recycled. Up until recently, PET could not be recycled in a closed loop, meaning back into its original purpose. (PET has been shredded, for example, for use as fiberfill in parkas and pillows). Also, recycled plastic was not technically feasible for food and beverages because of food safety laws. But new technology is changing all that.

In 1991, Coca–Cola announced the result of a several-year effort with its packaging supplier, Hoechst Celanese—the first plastic soft drink bottle made from 25% recycled PET. Pepsi-Cola, working with Goodyear, has also announced a 25% recycled PET container. Both have received FDA approval. With regard to potential health and safety concerns, a spokesperson for Coca-Cola reports there is "no downside to the use of recycled content from the consumer's perspective."[15] Meanwhile, both companies have found a way to demonstrate their environmental commitment, as well as preempt legislation.

Major consumer products marketers are upping their use of recycled content in plastic bottles for their household cleaning and laundry products. As just one example, bottles for Colgate's Palmolive dishwashing detergent are now made from 50% post-consumer recycled PET, a fact that is boldly emblazoned on product labels. In Australia, Palmolive liquid is available in 100% post-consumer PET.

In the plastic trash bag category, Webster Industries is stealing a lead on competitors with its Renew kitchen trash bags made from 100% recycled plastic, 30% of which is post-consumer material. A life cycle inventory has found that manufacturing the bags uses significantly less energy and resources and generates a fraction of the emissions that trash bags made with virgin plastic produce. Value priced at 25–30% less than leading brands Renew kitchen trash bags outsell Hefty in major markets, such as Philadelphia, San Francisco, and Chicago.[16]

CONSERVE NATURAL RESOURCES, HABITATS, AND ENDANGERED SPECIES

Teledyne has introduced a low-flow showerhead massage that enhances water efficiency by delivering the performance of a 7 gallon-per-minute shower at the low $2^1/_2$ gallon-per-minute rate now mandated in many states. Using a proprietary technology that helps to maintain the performance (pressure) of the water flow, Teledyne has managed to increase its already commanding market share lead.[17]

In Germany, AEG's "Lavamat" washing machine saves both water and energy and even comes with a special feature that helps to conserve on detergent. The innovation helped spare the company from bankruptcy.

The Knoll Group, a leading office furnishings manufacturer, is making its Gehry chair, a distinctive bentwood chair designed by world-renowned architect Frank Gehry, from maple obtained exclusively from the Menominee Tribal Forest. This forest, located in Wisconsin, has been certified by Scientific Certification Systems as sustainably managed; that is, the productive potential of the forest is being maintained while the native forest species, habitats, and indigenous people's land use rights are protected. While it is too early for sales results, the uniqueness of this effort has attracted significant press attention.[18]

MAKE PRODUCTS MORE ENERGY EFFICIENT

Philips' Earth Light compact fluorescent lightbulbs use 75% less energy and last 13 times longer than conventional bulbs. Over its lifetime, a compact fluorescent bulb will save $45 in electricity (or twice the cost of a bulb) while saving the energy equivalent of 500 lbs. of coal. Philips has found a unique sales opportunity in utilities who are giving the bulbs away or providing consumer rebates on the estimated $20 price.[19]

Twenty-five percent of water used in homes is heated. While many utilities provide rebates for energy-saving lightbulbs, a growing number are offering consumer purchase inducements for water-saving devices such as low flow showerheads and faucet aerators. One California retailer notes that sales of these high-margin items doubled when a local utility began offering such rebates.[20]

MAXIMIZE CONSUMER AND ENVIRONMENTAL SAFETY

In-use characteristics, especially those relating to personal health, are critical to consumers who shun products with chemicals perceived as a threat to personal health. This "chemophobia" will likely grow with the increased attention that's expected for the long-term effects of illness such as environmental chemical sensitivity and indoor pollution. Marketers are finding ways to eliminate some of the negatives associated with their products, thereby increasing consumer appeal while meeting legislative pressures.

Rather than put a state-mandated warning label on its product, Gillette reformulated its Liquid Paper line of correction fluids, substituting a different solvent for the carcinogenic trichloroethylene (TCE), while removing lead, which causes birth defects, and making other changes. The reformulation actually improved product performance. The product was relaunched as new and improved.[21]

Many household cleaning products contain chemicals such as chlorine and phosphates which are perceived to pollute lakes and streams when washed down the drain and pose risks to health. These concerns are creating volume opportunities for alternative cleaning products.

Heinz has introduced Heinz Cleaning Vinegar into test markets and and Miles Labs, makers of S.O.S. scouring pads, introduced into test markets in 1991 its Kitchen Safe household cleaner "for those consumers who are concerned about using conventional all-purpose cleaners on surfaces where food is stored or prepared." The formula includes lemon oil and baking soda to help cut grease and remove common household soil.[22]

In Europe, a little green frog is stirring up trouble for marketers of leading household cleaning products. In 1985, the Germany-based Werner & Mertz introduced the Green Frog line of environmentally sound household cleaners. The line consists of vinegar cleanser, natural cleanser, toilet cleanser, dishwashing liquid, window cleanser, scrubbing lotion, liquid detergent, and water softener. The line accounted for a whopping $300 million in sales in 1991.

Advertising Age reports that compared to the multimillion dollar television campaigns used by rivals, Green Frog cleansers have been supported by a $2 million advertising budget. Attention-getting, quirky one-third page ads feature a little green frog who's an expert on the environment and housework.

Green Frog's consumer appeal has caught major competitors such as Unilever, Procter & Gamble, Henkel, and Colgate-Palmolive by surprise. In Germany, the Green Frog brand has captured 16% of the $172 million market for household cleansers and become Germany's No. 3

cleanser behind P&G's Meister Proper (Mr. Clean) and Colgate's Ajax. Green Frog is also the No. 3 dishwashing liquid and ranks second and fourth in the toilet cleansers and window cleansers, respectively. It has been rolled out in nine other European countries including France, Spain, Italy, Finland, Denmark, Austria, Switzerland, Belgium, and the Netherlands.[23]

Ecover, an all-natural, concentrated laundry detergent and line of household cleaning products imported from Belgium, is formulated without phosphates, petroleum-based surfactants, artificial colors and perfumes, optical brighteners, enzymes, or chlorine bleach. Now enjoying growing distribution in health food stores in the United States, the environmentally positioned Ecover entered the U.K. in 1988 and quickly racked up a 1.5% share of the $1.8 billion market.[24]

MAKE PRODUCTS MORE DURABLE

While durability has historically been a consumer benefit for major appliances and automobiles, it will increasingly become a source of value-added and an indicator of quality and convenience in many other categories.

Maytag Washers and Volvo Cars have long been promoted as durable. In Europe, Volvo is currently leveraging this benefit with an environmental twist.

MAKE PRODUCTS AND PACKAGING REUSABLE OR REFILLABLE

Re-use has long been a factor in the U.S. marketplace, but has fallen out of favor with the onslaught of disposables. However, with legislative pressure on marketers to reduce packaging solid waste, reuse and refill strategies may enjoy renewed popularity.

Kraft General Foods' Good Seasons salad dressing mix has always used a refill notion. Consumers mix packaged dry seasonings with their own oil and vinegar into a free glass cruet. The brand's long-standing advertising theme, "Tastes fresh because you make it yourself," underscores the consumer benefits.

Concern over the environmental impact of disposable diapers, coupled with the introduction of more convenient cloth diaper products including ones with Velcro closures are two factors giving a boost to cloth diaper services, up 42% in 1990 over 1989.[25]

Gillette's Sensor razor, with 15% share of the $902 million North America blade market, proves that consumers will trade up from disposables to higher-price systems. The innovation has helped to enhance Gillette's leadership in shaving technology.[26]

Rubbermaid is taking advantage of the opportunity to help consumers reduce waste via the introduction of its Litterless Lunchbox, a reusable lunch box with special containers that can replace drink boxes, aluminum foil, and other wrappings.

DESIGN PRODUCTS FOR REMANUFACTURING, RECYCLING, AND REPAIR

In 1991, 45 product disposal bans were enacted by 12 states for such items as lead-acid batteries, tires, used oil, yard waste, and large appliances. Legislative pressures such as these are creating a need for manufacturers to design their products for remanufacture, recycling, and repair. Indeed, these attributes may be perceived as benefits to consumers looking to cut down on waste and save money. Marketers who design their products for recycling also need to help develop the collection infrastructure so that these products will, in fact, be recycled. Remanufactured models help consumers save money over purchasing a new model. A long-time strategy of the jet engine industry, design for remanufacturing may become an increasingly attractive option for manufacturers of major appliances who will be under increasing pressure to keep their bulky products out of dwindling landfills.

About 75% of a typical automobile consists of metals that are already being recycled. Now automakers are starting to tackle the remaining 25% known as "fluff" that consists of plastics, rubber, glass, fluids, and fabrics, which are the most difficult to recycle.

In 1990, the German-based Volkswagen AG preempted a law requiring that an infrastructure for automobile recycling be in place by 1994 and became the first automaker in the world to set up a pilot program to recycle scrap cars. Also in Germany, BMW has designed a car for disassembly and recycling. Its plastic parts are coded for recycling, and after fluids are drained, the car is disassembled. Components are categorized, sorted, and either rebuilt or recycled. New plastic parts are made from old ones; unusable parts are incinerated for energy.[27]

In January 1992, BMW of North America announced plans to start a similar pilot recycling program with the Automotive Dismantlers & Recyclers Association. The company plans to combine recycling with marketing incentives to sell new cars. During the first phase of the program, BMW will offer a $500 discount on a new purchase when owners return their worn-out BMWs to authorized recycling centers. The company is optimistic about the program's ability to reinforce a positive image with consumers. Rich Brooks, a spokesman for BMW, says vehicle recycling isn't yet a popular buying consideration but notes that, "people who buy our products are predisposed to environmental concerns and (are) apt to do something about it."[28]

In addition to glass, Heinz ketchup bottles are now made from PET and the company is working with local municipalities to spur the development of recycling programs.

TAKE PRODUCTS BACK FOR RECYCLING

As Exide has already discovered (see Chapter 3), retrieving used products and packaging, either directly from consumers or indirectly through the initiation of in-store collection programs, can provide a cost effective supply of material that can be turned into new products. It can also pay off in enhanced customer loyalty and deepened relationships with vendors.

In 1991, in anticipation of state legislation requiring battery manufacturers to reformulate products or set up collection programs for batteries containing heavy metals, Sanyo introduced rechargeable batteries in a container that doubles as a mail-back pack for recycling. When they return the batteries, consumers receive a $3 coupon good on their next purchase, and Sanyo gets a rare opportunity to hold on to its customer indefinitely. According to Richard Whitt, sales and marketing director for Sanyo's consumer energy products division, "Our focus groups told us we should be recycling. They also told us a company that does this will get some benefit."[29]

In 1992, First Brands, makers of Prestone anti-freeze, announced plans to introduce the first anti-freeze recycling program. Referring to used anti-freeze as "a valuable resource," the company sees an extensive system in which consumers, auto dealerships, service stations, heavy-duty fleet operations, and quick-lube facilities could drop off their old anti-freeze at special locations. Representing a potentially lucrative new business opportunity, the company plans to sell franchises for the preparation of anti-freeze for reuse at service station and other car-care locations.[30]

Do-it-yourself auto mechanics pour 190 million gallons of used motor oil into sewers and drains each year—more than 10 times the amount of oil spilled by the Exxon Valdez in 1989. Given that just one gallon of used motor oil can pollute one million gallons of fresh water, some states now require that service stations accept used motor oil from consumers. Mobil is just one oil refiner that is now accepting used engine oil at its service stations.[31]

In February 1992, Kodak announced a comprehensive recycling program designed to help retailers and photographic processing labs manage their solid photographic waste in an economical and environmentally sound way. By arranging for reduced cost collection and the recycling of specified photographic solid waste, the program will reduce photofinishers waste disposal fees, while enhancing their ability to comply with environmental regulation. Notes Robert F. Bell, manager of environmental programs for Kodak's consumer imaging division, "Individual labs have found it difficult to locate recyclers. The film container recycling program makes regional recycling centers available to every lab and simplifies the efforts for retailers and finishers. . . . Retailers will benefit from public perception of their participation in such an environmentally beneficial program." Retailers will encourage consumers to return film canisters with their processing for placement into the recycling stream.[32]

The music industry has decided to eliminate longbox compact disc packages by 1993; however, some record stores have begun recycling the containers until the new standard takes effect. At Tower Records, which operates 70 record stores nationwide, participating stores fill a 20-gallon bin with longboxes three to four times weekly. At some stores, managers report that 60 to 80% of their customers return because of the program. Moreover, 80% of the stores reduced their garbage collection costs by an average of $400 monthly through a combination of recycling efforts. The Sherman Oaks (Los Angeles) store, for example, which recycles office and computer paper, cardboard, and CD boxes, cut its fees by $600 monthly.[33]

MAKE PRODUCTS AND PACKAGING SAFE TO LANDFILL OR INCINERATE

Alkaline batteries, button batteries, rechargeable batteries, and automotive batteries contain hazardous heavy metals such as mercury, silver, nickel, cadmium, and lead that can eventually seep into underground water supplies. When these batteries are incinerated, heavy metals pollute the air or remain in ash that is then landfilled. Batteries must now meet strict mandates to reduce these pollutants. In 1990, Eveready met regulatory standards for mercury content 2 years ahead of schedule and was able to steal an edge on competitors through trade advertising.

MAKE PRODUCTS COMPOSTABLE

A strategy holding much promise for the 60% of organic waste that now clogs our landfills, compostability is being vigorously pursued by disposable diaper manufacturers. Procter & Gamble is testing ways to turn used diapers mixed with other organic matter like food and yard waste into a useful soil conditioner. They are now working to develop a fully compostable diaper (plastic backsheets on current models are not compostable), and have pledged $20 million to help municipalities support composting facilities.

Ideas for Action

Use the following checklist to explore the myriad opportunities that exist for refining existing products or developing new ones that meet environmental imperatives and satisfy consumers' primary demands.

Raw Material Procurement

• Can we minimize the potential for our raw materials procurement process to avoid tropical deforestation? Land stripping? Oil spills?

• Can we use renewable resources or resources that are sustainably managed?

Manufacturing

• What steps can we take to prevent or otherwise reduce the production of hazardous waste in our manufacturing processes? Can we dispose of any hazardous materials in a more environmentally benign manner?

Use

• Can we redesign our product so as to make it more energy or resource efficient?

• Can we make our product safer or more pleasant to use?

After-use and Disposal

• Can we design our product to make it durable? Refillable? Reusable? Repairable? Remanufacturable? Rechargeable?

• Can we redesign our product or package so as to save space in landfills?

• Can we make our products and packaging safer to landfill or incinerate?

Other

• Does our product provide any legitimate *solutions* to environmental ills? For example, can it help save water? Help cut down on resource and energy use? Reduce waste?

Notes

1. Gillespie, Robert S., "The Environment: Opportunities for Responsible Business," presentation to the Association of National Advertisers, Oct. 28, 1991.

2. "Life Cycle Analysis and Complying with CONEG's Model Packaging Standards Legislation," Franklin Associates Ltd., April 1992.

3. Lehrburger, Carl, et al., Diapers: Environmental Impact and Life Cycle Analysis," conducted for the National Association of Diaper Services, Jan. 1991.

4. Werner, Frances A., Monsanto, quoted in "Product Life Cycle Analysis: A Strategic Approach," *Conservation Exchange*, National Wildlife Federation, Winter, 1991, p.5.

5. Telephone conversation with Jon Corcoran, Director of Communications, Earth's Best, Apr. 30, 1992.

6. *The Green Consumer Letter*, Apr. 1992, p.3, and correspondence with Lynda Grose, Esprit, May 4, 1992, and *In Business*, May/June 1992, p.19.

7. Telephone conversation with Barbara Hausner, Melitta USA, Inc., June 15, 1992.

8. *Green MarketAlert*, Sept. 1991.

9. Telephone conversation with Deborah Cross, Coca-Cola, Apr. 10, 1992.

10. S.C. Johnson, environmental newsletter, *Partners Working for a Better World*, Feb. 1992, p.10.

11. *Household and Personal Products Industry*, Jan. 1992, p.42, and Jennifer Lawrence "P&G Tries New Ultra Detergents," *Advertising Age*, Feb. 2, 1992, p.48.

12. S.C. Johnson, environmental newsletter, *Partners Working for a Better World*, Feb. 1992, p.10.

13. *Green Consumer Letter*, Mar. 1992.

14. Telephone conversation with Omar Khalifa, Apple Computers, March 1992.

15. Telephone conversation with Deborah Cross, Coca-Cola, Apr. 10, 1992.

16. Telephone conversation with Cynthia Drucker, Webster Industries, May 1992.

17. Telephone conversation with Linda McKamy, McKamy & Partners, Jan. 1992.

18. Telephone conversation with George Wilmont, Knoll Group, May 18, 1992.

19. Conversation with Gregg DeSilvo, Philips Lighting, June 11, 1992.

20. Brenny, Jan, "Make Room for Water Savers," *Hardware Age*, Apr. 1992, p.66.

21. Smith, Randolph B., "California Spurs Reformulated Products," *The Wall Street Journal*, Nov. 1, 1990.

22. Miles Lab company press release.

23. Mussey, Dagmar, "Green Frog Brand Prepares to Hop into Concentrated Market," *Advertising Age*, Apr. 27, 1992, p.I-38.

24. *Management Today*, June 1990, *Household and Personal Products Industry*, April 1992, p.21.

25. Telephone conversation with Kathy Mautz, National Association of Diaper Services, June 11, 1992.

26. *Advertising Age*, July 6, 1992, p.S–12.

27. *Ecosource*, Vol. 2, No. 2, 1991, p.14.

28. *Advertising Age*, Mar. 30, 1992, p.S–46.

29. Lipton, Terry, "Beating the Green Rap," *ADWEEK, Marketing Week*, Jan. 27, 1992, p.6.

30. Wald, Matthew L., "Anti-freeze Maker Develops Recycling Plan," *The New York Times*, Feb. 28, 1992, and *The Wall Street Journal*, February 27, 1992.

31. *The Public Pulse*, Nov. 1991, p.6; *The New York Times*, Mobil advertisement, Mar. 19, 1992.

32. Kodak press release, Feb. 6, 1992.

33. *Green Marketing Report*, Mar. 1992, p.32.

Chapter 6

HOW TO COMMUNICATE WITH CREDIBILITY AND IMPACT

Communicating the benefits of more environmentally sound products can be challenging, indeed, even daunting. Some marketers fear backlash. Others are concerned that the benefits may not be tangible—lower emissions at the factory cannot be seen, smelled, or touched by consumers. Using new strategies, however, many marketers are finding real opportunity in tapping into green consumer motivations, educating consumers on their products' environmental benefits, and building trust.

Communicating environmental benefits, whether accomplished through advertising, public relations, or retailer programs, offers great rewards. Establishing an environmental image for products can help increase sales and distribution, enhance product value, and ward off legislative threats. Because corporations today need to project an image of environmental responsibility, green products can often secure a boost in marketing support from within.

Some marketers with bona fide green products may opt not to communicate their product's greenness, preferring, for example, not to draw attention to changes that may appear to be insignificant or for other reasons represent the potential to invite criticism. While there is always risk of backlash from stakeholders if communications are not in sync with expectations, *not* communicating environmental soundness can present other risks. The competition might move forward if you choose not to. You may lose the potential for increased distribution among environmentally aware retailers. And consumers may assume—because you don't tout its greenness—that your product or packaging is not environmentally sound.

Conservative marketers are increasingly utilizing public relations tactics to communicate their messages. They rely on advertising to highlight a brand's primary benefits, while employing public relations to communicate what is usually a supplemental environmental benefit. The value of this approach is twofold: public relations provides third-party credibility and reduces the potential for backlash for what might appear to be a self-congratulatory message.

There are instances when environmental messages should not be communicated to consumers or other stakeholders. In general, green communications efforts work best when:

• Green product attributes are obvious, legitimate, and meaningful to a significant amount of consumers

• A product's environmental benefits are tangible, and can be clearly and simply communicated

• Individual brand efforts are reinforced by substantive corporate initiatives and progress.

Use the following strategies to project the environmental soundness of products that meet the above criteria while establishing credibility and avoiding the potential for backlash.

Empower People

Tap into consumers' desire to make a difference and to exert control by using advertising appeals and other communications that empower them to improve the quality of their lives and the environment. Demonstrate how your environmentally sound products and services can help them make a difference.

• Marcal Paper products underscores the environmental benefits of its recycled content paper products with an empowering advertising theme, "Paper from paper, not from trees."

• Communications for The Body Shop emphasize personal empowerment and health and well-being, not product superiority.

• Working Assets, a long-distance telephone service that contributes a small percentage of a customer's bill to environmental, social, and political causes, promises in its advertising, "Working Assets lets you make a world of difference." Acknowledging that the socially aware are a growing niche in the marketplace and that people are becoming more concerned about letting their money speak for them, Peter Barnes, president of Working Assets, sees his service appealing to those people who favor peace, human rights, economic justice, and a safer environment. Recognizing the activist nature of its customers, Working Assets provides Free Speech days, allowing members to make free calls to senators to support legislation and other issues, and offers to send a Citizen Letter to targeted decision makers for a $3 fee. Barnes explains the magic behind Working Assets: "[Our] company's goal is to make it easy to make a difference. [We] let people act in the privacy of their homes, when they're doing things they already do."[1]

• In what may represent the beginning of a long-term shift away from sales messages that prey upon consumers' feelings of inadequacy, television commercials in the U.K. for the Ecover line of all-natural cleaning and laundry products poke fun at conventional advertising that promises to make clothes "whiter than white." The brand's empowering notion: "Ecover washes righter."

Make It Personal

While resource and energy savings are empowering, appeals to a consumer's immediate self interest are even more so. All consumers want to protect their health, save money, and keep their homes and communities clean and safe. They also want to save time and effort.

A green product often imparts direct personal benefits to the consumer that are more motivating than saving the planet and other altruistic notions: refills save money, pollution controls protect property, natural cotton colors say "I'm fashionable." These types of benefits should be highlighted whenever possible. For years, natural gas was positioned as "clean energy," but this apparently did not motivate consumers as much as the prospect of saving money.

• Advertising for 3M's "Safest Stripper" water-based furniture stripper dramatizes the in-use benefits of its low-fume formula with a visual depicting a man in a gas mask ready to strip paint from furniture. The headline proclaims, "Now you don't have to dress up to strip anymore."

• Referring to money, gasoline, and the environment, introductory advertising for Honda's VX entices consumers with the appeal, "Think of what you can save."

• Introductory advertising for Procter & Gamble's Downy fabric softener refill made the dual promise of "Less money. Less waste." Current advertising directly links the environmental benefits to the brand's historical softness benefit: "So much softness. So little waste."

Acknowledge the Differences That Exist in Environmental Commitment of Consumers

The diversity of green interest that exists within the population suggests opportunities for communications and product positioning based on specific environmental attributes and pricing. As Roper has found, the degree to which people are engaged and active is largely determined by their sense of impact. The relatively lower level of environment-related behavior demonstrated by the Grousers and the Basic Browns reflects their feelings that their actions are meaningless. In contrast, activists feel empowered because they believe they can change things. The challenge for marketers is to understand the underlying motivations of their target market, empowering the disenfranchised as necessary and rewarding the behaviors of those consumers who are trying to make a difference. For example:

- Motivate True-Blue Greens by demonstrating how they can make a contribution. Reward their initiative, leadership, and commitment.

- Show Greenbacks that environmental benefits are consistent with busy lifestyles and thus add value to products.

- Encourage Sprouts with appeals to peer pressure, status, and doing the right thing.

- Provide Grousers with easy, cost-effective ways to make a contribution.

- Help Basic Browns understand how individuals can make a difference. Underscore that small actions when performed by many can make big changes.

The potential to motivate the large mass of passive greens with peer pressure cannot be overstated. Environmental issues are inherently social: your gas-guzzling car pollutes my air; my wastefulness clogs our landfill. Today, the "cool" people care about the environment—the influentials, whom everybody else emulates.

This dynamic underpinned a highly successful anti-litter campaign created for the state of Texas by Austin-based GSD&M advertising agency. When research showed that slogans like "Pitch In" were having no effect on habitual litterers (men 18–34), advertising enlisted popular Texas celebrities like Willie Nelson, Randy White of the Dallas Cowboys, and George Foreman to demonstrate that it is uncool to litter. In the first year alone, the "Don't Mess with Texas" campaign helped reduce visible roadside litter by 29%—well above the 17% goal. The number of littered beverage containers in Texas is now lower than that in states with deposit laws.

Be Upbeat and Positive

In keeping with the consumers' desire to enjoy a comfortable, worry-free life, stress prosperity and a better future for consumers and their children. Upbeat messages also provide the best chance of enlisting much-needed support from consumers for necessary behavioral changes.

Educate

Many environmentally sound products use technologies and materials that are new to consumers. Some environmentally sound products are more expensive to produce and market. So educational messages may be needed to help favorably dispose consumers to some green product purchases and help accelerate the acceptance of green products in general.

Seventh Generation:
An Education-Intensive Strategy at Work

Founders Alan Newman and Jeffrey Hollender have seized on an opportunity to attract consumers who are looking to do right by the environment. They have positioned their catalog of more than 300 environmentally preferable products (ranging from non-toxic cleaning products to solar-powered radios) as a resource guide that educates consumers about environmental problems and offers easy, practical solutions.

In unprecedented fashion detailed copy explains product-related environmental issues such as why some household cleaning aids can be hazardous to the environment and highlights the environmental benefits of products offered for sale. For example, the catalog explains that showers fitted with low-flow showerheads could save a family of four an estimated 12,264 gallons of water per year and $17–85 on hot water heating, depending upon whether they use natural gas or electric heat. Recognizing that environmentally aware consumers have insatiable appetites for information on the issues, Seventh Generation provides a highly accessible consumer hotline service, a monthly newsletter, and has even published a more sophisticated guide on environmentally responsible shopping entitled, *Is It Really Green?*

This education-intensive strategy is paying off in both sales and customer loyalty. Seventh Generation's sales have reached to $10 million in just 3$1/2$ years.

According to Newman, Seventh Generation's president, the education-intensive strategy removes major obstacles to purchasing new types of products and technology that sometimes require behavioral changes. He explains, "If we share the information, people realize what is the logical choice. It helps people make the same choice we made."

Education Key to the Launch of GM's Impact

The communications strategy for the 1995 launch of General Motors' Impact electric car is already in development. With an entire new technology at hand, education will be critical. The communications strategy for Impact will be to educate consumers before media advertising begins. Explains Amy Rader, director of advertising for GM's electric vehicles: "The way I see this working, the education is going to start out teaching people what electric vehicles are, teaching people what questions to ask so they can start comparing. We have to give consumers a start on how to compare alternative fuels. The second step is to teach people how to realistically look at their driving patterns to see if an electric car is right for them.

When they stop, how long do they stop? Is it long enough to recharge? Getting people to start thinking about their own needs is going to be an important part of our job.'' As the vehicle gets close to production, the task of advertising will be to convince people to buy GM's product.

GM knows that consumers won't buy a car based on environmental benefits alone, so the sales pitch will focus on the convenience aspects of owning a car that is virtually maintenance free and can be refueled at home rather than at a gas station.[2]

Provide Performance Reassurance

Some environmentally preferable products, such as compact fluorescent lightbulbs and ethanol blend gasoline, perform differently from the products they are designed to replace and thus may be perceived as less effective. Northville, an oil refiner based in Long Island, New York, overcame this problem with a statement on behalf of its 10% ethanol blend clean air gasoline: "General Motors and all other automobile manufacturers support and approve the new clean air gasolines." At one point, ARCO considered positioning its EC–1 gasoline as a whole new type of fuel named Arcoline. However, they decided on EC–1 reformulated gasoline when consumer feedback showed fear of putting an untried fuel in the tank.[3]

Establish Credibility and Avoid the Backlash

Even for the most thoroughly researched products and advertising, it is not easy to establish credibility or avoid backlash. Criticism can come from many sources: environmentalists, media, customers, competitors, and the scientific community. While no marketer wants to face the possibility of criticism, *not* moving ahead may be even more detrimental. Extraordinary efforts have the potential to reap big rewards. ARCO's plan for the introduction of their Emission Control gasoline demonstrates many of the possibilities.

ARCO Emission Control Gasoline: A Case Study in Credibility

When preparing to introduce its emission control gasolines, ARCO realized it would have to get over the hurdle of credibility. Consumers just don't trust oil companies' gasoline claims. ARCO knew that to create acceptance for the new gasoline the advertising had to be credible, without puffery or overpromise. At the same time, it had to be heroic enough to portray the technological breakthrough of this new gasoline, as well as the potential long-term benefits. The advertising campaign was divided into three phases: introductory, sustaining, and results. It was launched in TV, radio, print, and outdoor ads in Los Angeles and San Diego in Fall, 1989.

In the introductory phase, the advertising dramatized the current and future benefits of EC–1 gasoline for consumers and the environment. The single most important element of credibility in the advertising was highlighting the benefit through the use of a substantiated claim. The claim was based on a computer model developed by ARCO and the South Coast Air Quality Management District (SCAQMD), the local regulatory board, after thorough testing of the new fuel. With these test results they were able to project the total pollution reductions if everyone who could use the fuel actually did use it. For added credibility, both the California Air Resources Board (CARB) and the South Coast Air Quality Management District (SCAQMD) were asked to approve the claim prior to the launch of advertising.

They acknowledged that this fuel did not represent the *ultimate* solution, but it was part of the solution. Long copy print ads, run during the sustaining phase, explained that EC–1 represented just one part of AR-

CO's corporate commitment to reducing pollution. To further promote its positive image, corporate advertising highlighted the many steps consumers could take to reduce air pollution—including using EC–1.

The results phase of the campaign showed consumers how they were making a difference when they purchased EC–1 gasoline. Advertising celebrated a SCAQMD report that L.A.'s air in 1990 was the cleanest it had been in 40 years. ARCO thanked customers for preventing over 100 million pounds of emissions from further polluting the air.

Although not a primary company objective, ARCO's position as a leader in the development of clean fuel has clearly had a major impact on its consumer image. Research shows that ARCO is clearly viewed more positively than all other oil companies. In the meantime, ARCO gasoline sales have increased 17%.[4]

ARCO's efforts suggest these strategies for establishing credibility and avoiding the backlash.

BE A LEADER

The first one into the marketplace reaps the lion's share of the rewards. A host of reformulated fuels have been introduced since EC–1 gasoline, but it is ARCO that gets the positive halo for pioneering a solution for cleaner air.

COMMUNICATE GREEN PRODUCTS AS PART OF A CORPORATE POLICY OF ENVIRONMENTAL EXCELLENCE

While reformulated gasoline reduces emissions compared to regular gasoline (especially leaded gas used by older cars), alternatives such as electric cars do exist. Consumers understand situations like this. While demanding high standards from industry, they expect progress rather than perfection. Thus, as ARCO discovered, credibility can be gained by positioning one's message as an evolutionary step toward achieving an overall corporate goal of environmental excellence. Introductory advertising positioning EC–1 as "Part of the Solution" promised that "We're not stopping here," and set forth objectives for future improvements.

In a similar vein, advertising supporting the Chemical Manufacturers Association's (CMA) Responsible Care campaign explained that "Since 1987, we've cut the amount of waste we release to water by 56%. Clearly, we're only part way there." For added credibility, the CMA advertisement includes a toll-free number to help consumers track progress of chemical companies in their area and helps them find needed answers. The advertising is themelined, "We want you to know."

Apple positioned its move to unbleached fiberboard shipping cartons as a sign of ongoing corporate commitment to the environment. An understated notice inserted into the cartons say:

> Apple is committed to being environmentally responsible. Changing our box color from white to brown is one step we've taken to reduce pollution and increase the use of recycled materials. Over the coming months and years, you can expect to see more progress as we continue to discover ways to care for the environment. For more information, please contact the Apple Customer Assistance Center at 1-800-776-2333.

HIGHLIGHT PRODUCT DIFFERENCES AND ACHIEVEMENTS. DON'T OVERPROMISE, EXAGGERATE, OR MISLEAD

ARCO's EC–1 gasoline offered a significant 20% decrease in emissions. Following its principle of "activism before communication," Patagonia, the outerwear manufacturer, donates 10% of pre-tax profits to environmental groups and did so for four years before including a statement—in small print—about such efforts in its catalog. Marketers can avoid potential criticism for advertising that may overstate achievements by heeding these words of Frederick Elkind, senior vice president of Ogilvy & Mather Advertising: "When it comes to the environment, underpromise and overdeliver."

Inconsistency in labeling laws across individual states creates a difficult situation for marketers of nationally distributed products. Until uniform guidelines are promulgated, marketers should adhere to the most stringent laws that apply to the states in which they distribute their products. Also, to ensure that environmental claims are helpful to consumers while minimizing risks of liability, marketers can follow voluntary guidelines issued for this purpose by the FTC in July 1992. The full guidelines can be obtained from the FTC in Washington, D.C. The guidelines are paraphrased here:

Be Clear and Prominent

When making environmental claims, be sufficiently clear and prominently displayed to prevent deception. This includes clarity of language, relative type size, and proximity of the claim to its qualifiers.

Distinguish Between Product and Package Benefits

Present environmental marketing claims in a way that makes clear whether the environmental attribute or benefit being asserted applies to the product, the package, or a component or portion of either. An example includes: "Packaging made from 25% post-consumer recycled content."

Do Not Overstate

Avoid vague, trivial, or irrelevant claims that can create a false impression of a product's overall environmental soundness. Broad labels such as "ozone-safe" or "ozone friendly" should be qualified so as to prevent consumer deception about the specific nature of the environmental benefit being asserted. For example a claim that would likely be acceptable under the FTC guidelines includes: "Contains no CFC propellants which are known to deplete the earth's upper ozone layer." Other environment-related terms that need to be qualified include: degradable/biodegradable/photodegradable, compostable, recyclable, made from recycled content, source reduction, reusable/refillable.

The term *degradable*, for example, should be qualified to avoid consumer deception about the potential for a product or package to degrade in the likely disposal site, as well as the rate and extent of degradability. Thus, the term should be substantiated with competent and reliable evidence that the entire product or package will completely decompose into natural elements within a reasonably short period of time after the product is disposed of in the customary way. Similarly, claims relating to recyclability should be qualified so as to avoid misleading consumers as to a product's or package's potential recyclability. Thus, a claim such as "recyclable" would be prohibited in areas where consumers do not have access to recycling for the particular material. A qualified claim such as "This product is potentially recyclable, however, less than 10% of the U.S. population has access to recycling facilities for this type of material," would most likely be deemed in accordance with the FTC guidelines.

The importance of adhering to individual state laws—which the FTC guidelines do not preempt—cannot be overstated. For example, New York state requires that claims of recycled content meet minimum percentages of pre- and post-consumer material by weight whereas the FTC guidelines do not distinguish between pre- and post-consumer material.

Provide Complete Information

When making claims in which a comparison is made to the environmental benefits of a competitor's product, provide enough information so that consumers can make relevant decisions. Make sure the basis for comparison is sufficiently clear and is substantiated. ARCO's claim, backed up by scientific test results, provides a good model: "reduced emissions 20% versus regular leaded gasolines."

ENLIST THE SUPPORT OF TRUSTED THIRD PARTIES

A key to the success of advertising for ARCO's EC–1 gasoline was opening lines of communications with the local regulatory boards. Those agencies supported the reformulated gasoline and thus helped to protect ARCO from the wrath of potential skeptics and critics who favored purer solutions such as electric cars and alternative-fuel vehicles.

Outside of regulators, third-party support can come in many forms: environmental groups (as in the case of Heinz' CEO consulting with Earth Island Institute prior to announcing a switch to dolphin-free tuna fishing methods—see Chapter 4); private consulting organizations that can perform independent life cycle inventories (See Chapter 5.), and organizations that certify claims and award "seals of approval" to be used on package labeling and in advertising. Certification organizations are discussed later in this chapter.

KEEP YOUR MESSAGES CONSISTENT WITH THE GOAL OF PROMOTING RESPONSIBLE CONSUMPTION

The ARCO EC–1 introduction was accompanied by corporate advertising in which consumers were asked to "help in the fight to save the air in Southern California" by taking measures such as eliminating unnecessary trips, ride sharing, and walking whenever possible."

Representing the ultimate in credibility building, Esprit ran an ad in 1990 in its catalog and a small circulation magazine that reaches influential consumers, headlined: "A Plea for Responsible Consumption." The ad asked consumers "(not to) buy anything you don't need, including our products." Esprit received hundreds of letters from consumers as young as 8 years old lauding the effort, and letters still arrive at the firm's San Francisco headquarters. Quincy Tompkins, who runs the Eco-desk at Esprit notes: "It won the respect from our consumers, that's for sure."

COOPERATE WITH OTHERS IN YOUR INDUSTRY

Work with competitors to promote industry-specific initiatives and share resources and technology. An important aspect of ARCO's successful introduction of EC-1 reformulated gasoline is that ARCO offered to share its formulation with competitors. Since ARCO only markets on the West Coast and has just one refinery dedicated to producing reformulated gasoline, sharing the recipe with others allowed the product benefits to be made broadly available.

CONSIDER THE ENVIRONMENTAL IMPACT OF YOUR MARKETING METHODS

Beyond environmental messages, consumers are increasingly scrutinizing the medium in which they are placed. How many readers looked to see if this book was printed on recycled paper? Underscore your credibility by using media vehicles with environmentally acceptable paper content, recyclability, etc.

The direct marketing industry is under fire due to consumer perceptions of catalogs and other third-class mail as wasteful. Legislative pressures are mounting in some states to use recycled materials. Recognizing the environmental impacts of its direct mail campaign, Working Assets is sure to use only recycled paper. Marketing director Robin Greiner reports, "We figure out how many trees were used (for each mailing) and we plant more." The Seventh Generation catalog only uses recycled paper and customers can specify how many catalogs they want to receive each year. Apple Computer's carton insert, appropriately, is printed on unbleached recycled-content paper.

The developers of Keyes Fibre's Chinet Environmental Experiment chose recycled paper for both the printing paper and the folder it was placed in, and printed on both sides of the paper using minimum impact inks. Packaging was kept to a minimum and a padded shipping bag made from 60% recycled content was chosen. Explains Judy Meyenhofer, one of the developers, "If you're going to do something like this, you must consider all aspects from start to finish, because if you don't, no one will believe you."

CONSIDER INDEPENDENT CLAIM CERTIFICATION

No eco-labeling program akin to those in Germany, Canada, or Japan exists in the United States. However, two independent non-profit environmental testing organizations now exist to serve the need for a third-party review of manufacturer claims and to support the market for environmentally sound products. These organizations are Green Seal, based in Washington, D.C., and Scientific Certification Systems of Oakland, CA.

Green Seal, founded in 1990 by a coalition of environmentalists and other interested parties, seeks to provide a "seal of approval" for products which it deems better for the environment in various product categories. Companies pay to have their products reviewed, and then pay an annual licensing fee to use the seal on product labeling. All products in a category that meet the standards are eligible for the seal. As of this writing, the group has finalized standards for lightbulbs, recycled motor oil, and toilet tissue made from recycled content among other product categories, and has begun to accept applications from manufacturers.

Scientific Certification Systems (SCS) was founded in 1984 to detect pesticide residues on produce. It now also certifies specific environmental claims and, as mentioned earlier, conducts life cycle inventory studies for those companies who wish to have their products judged on a comprehensive environmental basis. Rather than issuing a seal of approval, SCS provides a detailed environmental report card, more along the lines of nutritional labeling. The group has certified over 500 specific claims for 150 companies including Apple Computer, Clorox, and Glidden.

While it is still too early to ascertain the sales impact of these independent certification programs, the benefits outside of direct sales may suggest their consideration:

• Independent certification programs reinforce a corporation's environmental commitment and help establish credibility with consumers, media, and environmental groups.

• With fierce competition for consumer loyalty, a product label bearing a certified claim or seal of approval could represent a potential source of competitive advantage.

• Independent certifications or seals of approval can enhance distribution through environmentally aware retailers and especially those, like the Home Depot, which require vendors to submit their environmental claims to third parties for review.

Research conducted by J. Walter Thompson in 1991 suggests a potential benefit among consumers of enlisting the support of these organizations. When asked what type of guarantee would increase their confidence in the environmental safety of a product, consumers chose third parties such as environmental groups and independent laboratories. (See Exhibit 6.1.)

While third parties such as Good Housekeeping and Underwriters Laboratories (UL) have historically helped to enhance the credibility of manufacturers' claims, avid support for environmental groups and independent laboratories indicates a strong potential role for these fledgling independent environmental testing organizations.

Studies show that about 80% of consumers claim that their buying decisions would be influenced by presence of a seal, but the potential for sales is perhaps best reflected in the words of one respondent in a focus group conducted by J. Walter Thompson in 1990. Upon viewing SCS's Green Cross on a product label she said, "It wouldn't make me buy it, but I would definitely pick it up off the shelf and read a little bit about it."

Positive experiences with government-sponsored programs in many countries of the world (See Chapter 1.) suggest a bright future for these U.S. programs or ones that could potentially be developed by the government.

EXHIBIT 6.1
Guarantees to Enhance Confidence in the Environmental Safety of a Product

Approval from a well-known environmental group	39%
Independent laboratory approval	28
Scientists testimonial	19
Manufacturer's warranty	9

Source: J. Walter Thompson, *Greenwatch*, No. 3, Spring/Summer 1991.

Ideas for Action

Ask the following questions to evaluate opportunities to add credibility and impact to your environmental communications.

• Legitimate solutions to environmental ills? Which does our product or package provide? For example, does it save energy, reduce waste, or dispose safely?

• Are our claims consistent with the laws that may exist in the states where we distribute?

• Can we communicate our message without the risk of misleading consumers?

• Are our environmental benefits worthy of third party certification?

• Are the print media in which we advertise or promote using recycled paper?

Notes

1. Goerne, Carrie, "Reach Out and Change the World: Long Distance Service Helps Users Make a Difference the Easy Way." *Marketing News,* Mar. 16, 1992, p.10.

2. Frame, Phil, "Battery Powers' Impact Takes Hold at GM," *Advertising Age*, Mar. 20, 1992, p.S-34.

3. Kresser, Robert, presentation to *Advertising Age* "Green Marketing West" Conference, Oct. 31, 1991.

4. Kresser/Craig Case Study, "ARCO Emission Control Gasolines," Kresser/Craig Advertising, Santa Monica, CA.

Chapter 7

PUTTING IT ALL TOGETHER

The new strategies required to reap the opportunities of environmental consumerism are numerous and far reaching. They not only represent a shift in communications strategies, but a new approach to product development and the ability to forge constructive coalitions with a wide array of corporate environmental stakeholders. Taken together, these strategies reinforce each other so as to shape a thorough and credible response to consumers' environmental concerns. Using them in concert provides marketers with the best chance to reap the many rewards of green. While the environmental consumerism trend is still in its infancy, there is much to be learned from pioneering companies who utilize many of these strategies as a matter of course and are reaping the benefits. It is these companies that we turn to in this chapter.

While many companies both large and small fit into this category—Patagonia, Stride Rite, and Ben & Jerry's to name a few—two have been chosen to be profiled in depth: Church & Dwight and Tom's of Maine. In business for over 150 and 20 years respectively, Church & Dwight and Tom's of Maine prove that environmental strategies can form the basis of an enduring business and provide leverage in the face of formidable competition. They superbly demonstrate the new marketing strategies at work. These strategies are summarized at the close of this chapter.

Church & Dwight: Green on the Inside as Well as the Outside

The granddaddy of green marketers, Church & Dwight has been environmentally conscious throughout its entire 150-year history. The company's flagship product, Arm & Hammer brand baking soda, is one of the greenest products to be found in the supermarket. Baking soda is made from sodium bicarbonate, a naturally occurring mineral. Composed of bicarbonate and sodium ions, both of which are present in the human body, baking soda is one of the few products that can be used for internal consumption, personal care, and simple household cleaning.

Church & Dwight is a conservatively managed company that today is run by the fifth generation of the Dwight family. They were pioneers in the conservation movement, having put trading-type conservation cards depicting various bird species in its boxes from 1888 until 1966. Long before Rachel Carson's landmark book *Silent Spring* was published in 1962, drawing a link between the use of pesticides such as DDT and a declining bird population, Church & Dwight's conservation cards carried the slogan, "For the good of all, do not destroy the birds." Since 1907, Church & Dwight has also used recycled paperboard for its yellow baking soda boxes.

Church & Dwight's modern day environmental initiatives started in 1970 with sponsorship of the first Earth Day. At the same time, they introduced Arm & Hammer laundry detergent, America's first national phosphate-free brand of powder laundry detergent. The product, made primarily from sodium carbonate, quelled mounting public concern about the run-off of phosphates which were linked to clogged waterways and algae growth that deprived marine life of oxygen. Another of the company's consumer products is Arm & Hammer Dental Care, the country's largest selling brand of baking-soda toothpaste.

Recognizing that corporate environmental reputations must be earned, Church & Dwight has now embarked on an extensive internal greening program that they refer to as the Environmental Improvement Process (EIP). This corporate program consists of a two-pronged, balanced approach to environmentalism: an internal focus on compliance and prevention, and external outreach efforts emphasizing education and brand support. This combination, coupled with a 150-year-old corporate commitment to safeguarding the environment, is paying off in reduced costs, lessened environmental impact, and increased sales for the Arm & Hammer product line.

CORPORATE COMMITMENT STARTS AT THE TOP

At Church & Dwight, corporate commitment to environmental cleanup and pollution prevention starts at the top with Chairman Dwight Minton, who is an active member of the Greater Yellowstone Coalition, among other organizations. Policy is developed by a Corporate Environmental Task Force to which all employees are encouraged to submit suggestions. The company recognizes that environmental excellence is an ideal, rather than realistic goal since all corporate processes must impact the environment to some degree. Explains Bryan Thomlison, the firm's environmental affairs director, "Environmentalism at Church & Dwight is a process, not a program. We do it, refine it, and do it again."

To help integrate the program into the corporate culture, Church & Dwight's EIP has been folded into the company's ongoing Total Quality Management Program. It is supported by efforts designed to empower every employee with knowledge and the ability to be heard. Acknowledging that some efforts are bound to fail despite the best of intentions, Thomlison reminds his colleagues not to be afraid to learn from their mistakes.

OBJECTIVITY IS A KEY TO SUCCESS

Another key element of Church & Dwight's environmental strategy is obtaining objective information. So, in addition to conducting annual compliance audits and meeting the stringent regulations of the chemical industry's Responsible Care program of manufacturing and waste management guidelines, Church & Dwight has retained an outside firm to conduct an environmental quality audit of its offices, cafeteria, and other non-manufacturing facilities. The audit has not only uncovered potential areas for real environmental improvement, but has also found a number of ways to save the company significant sums of money through the use of energy-efficient lighting, two-sided photocopying, and other measures.

STAKEHOLDERS' ALLIANCES ARE KEY TO EXTERNAL OUTREACH

Church & Dwight's aggressive outreach program caters to the needs of a wide-ranging group of stakeholders composed of legislators, environmentalists, educators, industry associations, retailers, and the media.

As stated in the firm's environmental policy statement, "Building coalitions with all key stakeholders keeps the company abreast of environmental regulations, issues, debates, technology, and attitudes." Thomlison finds that "Building coalitions results in a dialogue that can lead to objectivity in the development of corporate and environmental stakeholder policies and practices." He adds, "From a marketing standpoint, building coalitions extends one's message to the most environmentally aware consumers and builds credibility." An important part of Church & Dwight's stakeholder program is sharing information and learning with other companies. This helps to establish a leadership image for Church & Dwight, while fostering good environmental practices—to the benefit of all—within the consumer products industry.

Church & Dwight's Corporate Environmental Plan includes a separate strategy and plan for each stakeholder group; programmatic efforts strive to build "win-win" situations for the company and its various environmental stakeholders.

Specific programmatic efforts conducted by Church & Dwight between 1989-1991 have included:

• Sponsorship of Earth Day 1990 (making it the only company in America to sponsor both the 1970 and 1990 Earth Day events)

• An educational program titled, "Partnerships in Environmental Education," which involve the efforts of many environmental stakeholder groups and includes educational outreach initiatives, such as:

1. Technical support for authors of environmental books and newsletters
2. A 65-part radio series that was written by three leading environmental organizations
3. A multimedia educational exhibit on sustainable development, entitled "Caring for Earth: Educating for a Sustainable Future." It was produced by Church & Dwight and co-sponsors the Good Housekeeping Institute and Target Stores for the United Nations Environmental Programme, UNESCO, and the United States Environmental Protection Agency.
4. A *Community Action Handbook* designed to empower local store owners with the motivation and skills to organize community-based environmental coalitions, modeled after Church & Dwight's national efforts
5. Support for the United States EPA-sponsored President's Environmental Youth Awards
6. Donations to local, state, and national environmental groups and causes
7. In-store merchandising programs such as "Enviro-centers" described in Chapter 4.

A key ingredient underlying the effectiveness of these diverse initiatives is that each involved, from concept through implementation, a coalition of environmental stakeholders. According to Thomlison, "Merging the complementary skills and resources made the programs bigger and better."

Church & Dwight's efforts and their longstanding commitment to the environment are serving them well. In the past 20 years, sales have grown from $16 million to almost $500 million, and the company is well positioned to benefit even more as the environmental consumerism trend becomes more entrenched. The R&D department continues to find lucrative new functions for baking soda or its carbonate-based brethren, including use as a non-toxic paint-stripping compound that works in a process similar to sandblasting (in fact, it was used in the restoration of the Statue of Liberty), as an aide to controlling acid rain-causing emissions from industrial smokestacks, and even in the reduction of lead in drinking water.

Church & Dwight has been recognized by prominent environmental groups for its efforts. It was given a Green Star Award from New York City's Environmental Action Coalition, and it has also received the Council of Economic Priorities' coveted Corporate Conscience Award, as well as the United Nations Environmental Programme's (UNEP) Earth Achievement Award for Environmental and Social Responsibility.

Tom's of Maine: Where Corporate Social Responsibility Is a Way of Life

The husband-and-wife team of Tom and Kate Chappell founded their Kennebunk, Maine, health and beauty aids firm in 1970. Their mission was to create products that were more healthful to use, and to produce those products in synergy with their community and environment.

The makers of the fast-growing Tom's of Maine brand toothpaste, deodorant, and mouthwash founded their company on the notion that humans, animals, and nature deserve respect and dignity. Their commitment to social responsibility is not taken lightly. According to Katie Shisler, the firm's director of creative services, "You have to mean it and live it. It influences every aspect of the way we do business, from how we listen to and respond to our consumers, how we treat our employees (flexible work schedules and job sharing are commonplace), to how we interact with the community, how we deal with our trading partners, how we deal with the environment, and, ultimately, how we share our profits."

Accordingly, the firm's products are made from the highest quality natural ingredients and do not contain additives, preservatives, artificial flavors, or fragrances. Products are also packaged responsibly. Tom's of Maine toothpaste comes in a recyclable aluminum tube inserted in a box made from 100% recycled cardboard and printed with soy-based inks. Shampoo is packaged in recycled plastic, and roll-on deodorants and antiperspirants are packaged in refillable and recyclable glass bottles.

Long before it was mandatory, Tom's of Maine listed ingredients on product labels. Tom's ingredient list also includes the specific purpose and source of each ingredient.

To reinforce its commitment to people, Tom and Kate Chappell's signatures appear on every product label. Each consumer letter is answered "Dear Friend." Says Shisler, "When you operate in the realm of friendship, you're in a different area of responsibility. A company goes beyond dollar sales to anticipate needs. Just as in a personal friendship, when we don't do something right, we say we're sorry and work to correct it."

The company takes its responsibility to the community seriously. Ten percent of pre-tax profits are donated to charitable causes, representing one of the highest percentage donations of any corporation in America. Seventy-five percent of that money is directed toward environmental concerns such as recycling and conservation. Last year, with financial support and the loan-out of an employee who affectionately became known as "The Trash Lady," the company helped the town of Kennebunk start its first recycling program. It has also formed a long-standing relationship (over 10 years) with a facility for the mentally and physically challenged and provides job opportunities for several of the group's clients.

At Tom's of Maine, a little respect for the consumer and a willingness to step beyond the mandate of regulation is paying off and likely will continue to in the future. Their offerings command a 20%–50% premium, depending on the product and market. The company has been growing at an annual rate of 25%–30%. In 1991, the company's sales were $16 million, double those of 1988.

What started as a profitable niche opportunity is now finding its way into the mainstream. The full line of Tom's of Maine brand health and beauty aids is now distributed in 7,000 health food stores throughout the US, Canada, and England, as well as 20,000 food and drug outlets on the East and West coasts.

Admittedly, Tom's of Maine's environmental and social strategies are not based sheerly on altruism. Shisler concedes, "The environmental playing field will be level in the future. Any businessperson who's paying attention knows when the field is leveled, consumers will go beyond packaging to ask, 'What's inside the box? Who makes this product?' Simply putting a recyclable label on a carton won't be enough. It's a critical first step but it will soon be status quo." She believes companies need to "walk the walk"—that is, how a company lives builds trust. She thinks consumers will recognize this, too, and say, "They deliver."

Indeed, Heidi Catano, communications manager, reports that the company receives over 150 letters a week from consumers. She notes the one theme that dominates the consumer mail is an appreciation for the kind of company Tom's of Maine is. This may be the company's greatest asset.

Now associated with at least six categories of health and beauty aids, the Tom's of Maine name is well on its way toward becoming a master brand, an image that provides new products with instant identification as socially and environmentally responsible. With a corporate image that larger consumer products companies envy, Tom's of Maine is well positioned to compete for consumer loyalty. Indeed this competitive advantage is already paying off: the company's toothpaste is fast becoming a number three or four brand in certain markets in the Northeast, Mid-Atlantic, and West Coast. In the years ahead, Tom's of Maine could well become a household name among discriminating consumers nationwide.

Ten Winning Strategies for Succeeding in the Age of Environmental Consumerism

1. Do Your Homework

- Understand the full range of environmental, economic, political, and social issues that affect your business.

2. Get Your House in Order

- Start with a commitment from the CEO

- Empower employees to develop environmentally sound products and processes

- Enlist the support of independent auditors

- Integrate environmental issues into your marketing planning

- Turn your brand managers into brand stewards

- Communicate your corporate commitment and project your values.

3. Be a Leader

- Be pro-active; set standards for your industry

- Foster cooperation among competitors.

4. Build Coalitions with Corporate Environmental Stakeholders

- Educate consumers on environmental issues and how to solve them, help teachers educate our young

- Work with legislators and government agencies to develop balanced legislation and regulations

- Share information with environmental groups and solicit their technical support

- Inform the media of your environmental initiatives

- Help retailers address consumer needs and reduce solid waste.

5. Develop Products That Balance Consumers' Needs

- Combine high quality, convenience, and affordable pricing with environmental soundness

- Minimize the environmental impact of products and packaging at every stage of the life cycle

- Take the high road. Strive to use leading edge technologies, materials, and design. Source reduce whenever possible.

6. Empower Consumers

- Help consumers understand the environmental benefits of your products and packaging

- Address the diversity of green. Reward the environmentally active and motivate passive consumers with easy, cost effective solutions.

7. Underpromise and Overdeliver on Your Environmental Marketing Claims

- Don't overstate, exaggerate, or mislead

- Use claims that are specific and supported by scientific evidence.

8. Establish Credibility

- Position product initiatives as part of your ongoing commitment to the environment

- Use third parties to add credibility and impact to your messages

- Promote responsible consumption.

9. Minimize the Environmental Impact of Your Marketing Programs

- Use recycled paper.

10. Think Long Term

- Monitor shifts in consumer attitudes, legislative trends, and changes in natural resources availability that could affect your business.

Epilogue

PREEMPTING
THE FUTURE

Noel Brown, North American director of the United Nation's Environmental Programme, has set an urgent tone for the 1990s. He warns, "We have 10 years left before environmental destruction is irreversible." Should we continue to utilize current technologies and energy forms in the face of global population growth, we may indeed threaten the planet's capacity for sustaining human life.

Fortunately, we can avoid what scientists and world leaders believe may be the inevitable by adopting technologies, materials, and energy forms that are *already in hand*. As environmental consultant Allan Martin Kaufman reminds us, "The problems of society have always been business's opportunities and business's responsibilities. No other segment of society has the will, the resources, the energy, the organization,

153

the imagination, or the vision." While some of the technologies or materials are not for various reasons, economic or political, in widespread use, golden opportunities are nevertheless present for marketers with vision and skill to tap these technologies to solve environmental problems. Particular opportunities lie in confronting issues related to solid waste and energy and water conservation.

One need only look to Germany, Holland, and other bellwether countries to see how existing technologies can help to create lifestyles and products that minimize environmental impact while setting standards for high quality, convenience, and affordability. Germany and Holland, for example, have environmentally attuned societies in which alternative transportation, organic food and clothing, source-reduced packaging, and other more environmentally sound technologies, products, and services have long been a way of life. Exhibit E.1 illustrates the comparison between U.S. environmental efforts and those of Germany and Holland.

EXHIBIT E.1
Germany and Holland Leading the Way

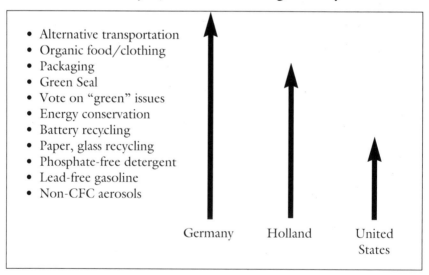

- Alternative transportation
- Organic food/clothing
- Packaging
- Green Seal
- Vote on "green" issues
- Energy conservation
- Battery recycling
- Paper, glass recycling
- Phosphate-free detergent
- Lead-free gasoline
- Non-CFC aerosols

Germany   Holland   United States

Source: The Sterling Group. Reprinted with permission.

According to the World Resources Institute, solving the problems of global environmental degradation will require:

• Stabilization of the population

• Transition to more efficient, environmentally sustainable technologies for manufacturing, energy production, transportation, and agriculture

• Elimination of subsidies on natural resources such as forests, energy, and water so as to promote conservation

• Necessary commitment of financial and technological resources to promote environmentally sound growth in developing countries.[1]

These solutions can occur only with a combination of international cooperation, changes in social and public policy, and new technologies. Herein lies the opportunity for industry. Technology already exists, or is in development, to help reverse major environmental problems such as global climate change and ozone layer depletion. In addition, products and materials already exist or are on drawing boards that enable consumers to maintain their high quality of life while maximizing use of natural resources and minimizing waste. Technologies already exist to promote alternative lifestyles that help to conserve energy as well as save people and businesses both time and money. For example:

• We know how to design homes that use energy sparingly; air conditioners, furnaces, refrigerators, and light fixtures that are from 50% to several times more efficient than their predecessors already exist.

• We know how to make construction materials and household furnishings that can reduce threats such as indoor air pollution.

• We know how to design our kitchens to make it easy for people to recycle and compost their waste.

• We know how to design plumbing systems that help to collect water that can be used to keep our lawns green and our gardens thriving.

• We know how to grow food using fewer chemical pesticides and fertilizers.

- We know how to raise cattle so as to use less water and less grain. We know how to grow alternative protein sources that use fewer resources overall.

Methods

Marketers of consumer products in the United States have particular opportunities to make a difference in five areas: alternative transportation, energy efficiency, conservation of water and other natural resources, solid waste management, and protection from environmental ills.

ALTERNATIVE TRANSPORTATION

With the levels of carbon dioxide emissions rising each year, global climate change is expected to be a key issue of the 1990s. Carbon dioxide, the gas released when fossil fuels are burned, is thought to be the single largest contributor to the problem. Major sources of carbon dioxide include pollution from factories, power generators, and automobiles.

Cars built since 1983 spew out significantly less pollutants than their pre-1983 counterparts. However, the total distance driven by automobiles has doubled in the United States since 1965.[2] While tremendous strides have been made, most of the technological gains have been offset by a growing population and usage of automobiles that not only continues to pollute the air, but creates congestion and degrades our land. An ecologically purer future necessitates fewer cars, and cars that are less polluting and more energy efficient.

In September 1990, the California Air Resources Board adopted a law that requires 2% of each automaker's sales to have zero emissions beginning in 1998, and the portion rises to 10% in 2003. As many as nine states and the District of Columbia have signed agreements supporting similar rules in their jurisdictions. Electric-powered cars are now on the roads, as are vehicles that operate on alternative fuels like methanol and compressed natural gas. Representing the great hope of the 21st century, the Japanese are funding a project to produce hydrogen, the cleanest burning of all fuels.

California air quality regulations also require that all companies with 100 or more employees act to reduce commuting miles. As a result, carpooling is practiced in companies such as 7-Up, Toshiba, and United Airlines, as are shortened work weeks. Government agencies appear to be setting the pace. At the South Coast Air Quality Management Board, for example, employees work a 4-40 week—four ten-hour days with three days off. These regulations may spur a larger trend toward teleconferencing, telecommuting, use of electronic mail, and electronic shopping.

The number of telecommuters (persons who work part or full time at home) is rising rapidly. There were an estimated 5.5 million telecommuters in the United States in 1991, up 38% over 1990.[3] In San Francisco, Scan Fone already allows busy people to pay bills and buy groceries using a special touch-tone phone, a bar code scanner, and a 6,000-item catalogue from Safeway Stores.[4] Telecommuting has already been shown to reduce air pollutants, save fuel, and improve employee morale.[5]

The Netherlands has pioneered the use of bicycles for personal transportation. The bicycle population (12 million) is close to total population (15 million). In Groningen, the largest city in the northern Netherlands, bicycles already account for half of all trips.[6] In the United States, a big opportunity exists to develop and market errand bikes—evolved forms of mountain bikes with wide tires and seats and collapsible metal baskets that could be used for short trips to the store. City policy in Greenfield, California, now calls for builders of new housing to provide two adult-sized bicycles free of charge with each home.[7]

To save money and cut down on pollution, suburbs and cities of the future may be designed around a town center within walking distance of homes. Cities may be clustered to eradicate urban sprawl.

ENERGY EFFICIENCY

Because of its links to the greenhouse effect, acid rain, and other problems, energy efficiency is a top environmental priority in the 1990s. Advanced energy efficient technologies and renewable energy sources such as solar power represent viable alternatives to fossil fuels. They can help cut carbon dioxide emissions and would help make our economy more competitive. For example, if we used energy as efficiently as Germany and Japan, we would be using half as much as we do now . Not only would we reduce air pollution substantially, we would save as much as $200 billion per year.[8]

In California, pioneering policies requiring no trade-off in consumers' quality of life have already improved energy efficiency, causing electricity use per person to decline 0.3% between 1978 and 1988, compared with an 11% increase in the rest of the United States.[9]

As Teledyne and Philips are discovering, opportunities abound to further develop consumer products that help promote energy savings and to promote them in concert with utilities. More than 20 state public utility commissions require their electric companies to promote and subsidize conservation by customers. Several utilities now provide free weatherization, free or subsidized distribution of more energy-efficient lightbulbs, and direct cash grants to residential and business customers who buy more efficient air conditioners and motors. The New England Electric System spent $120 million for these subsidies in 1991, and Con Edison of New York says it plans to spend more than $4 billion over the next 17 years.[10]

Long-term opportunities exist for advanced electronics that can monitor lighting and appliances, super-insulated refrigerators, and "smart windows" that can change their insulation value depending upon preset indoor temperatures; in the future, laws could require the installation of such devices to help alleviate the need to build additional power plants. Other opportunities exist to develop solar power. By one estimate, solar power could eventually provide 30% of the energy used in most countries.[11] Solar cells are being used to power calculators, radios, watches, and other small electronics that normally require batteries. In the future, opportunities may grow for solar-powered appliances. Auto air conditioners powered by rooftop solar panels are under development.

While originally introduced to help prevent fabric from shrinking in hot water, cold water detergents such as Cold Power and Woolite may experience an increase in sales as consumers become aware of the energy savings they can produce. Other cold-water based cleaning aids may one day join them on supermarket shelves.

CONSERVATION OF WATER AND OTHER NATURAL RESOURCES

In the United States, water is being pumped out of the ground at a rate 25% faster than it is being replenished. Dwindling water supplies are now legend in the West. By the year 2000, water supplies are projected to be inadequate in 16% of the country. Statistics compiled by Green Seal show that approximately 70% of water flushed down traditional-sized toilets isn't required for effective sewage transport, and 50% of the water used to shower isn't necessary either. According to the group, the wasted water is enough to supply the annual needs of more than 80 million Americans.[12]

With a population that could double to 500 million (or half the size of China) in the next 80 years, water conservation is destined to become a critical societal issue. To help us meet the challenges, advanced plumbing systems that utilize "gray water" (the used water from showers and sinks that is then filtered to run the toilets and water the lawn) are being tested for residential use in drought-ridden Santa Monica, California. In New Jersey, a large office building has cut water consumption by 62% through the use of an on-site treatment and reuse system, and sanitation districts near Los Angeles are saving 60 million gallons per day by reclaiming water and using it for irrigation, industrial cooling, and other purposes.

Representing other substantial sources of long-term water savings, efforts are underway to develop "dry" washing machines that use sound waves to clean clothes. Xeriscaping—landscaping with native shrubs and flowers—may one day replace conventional lawns. Xeriscaping not only saves water, it helps to cut down on the use of chemical pesticides and fertilizers.

Resource-Efficient Food Production

According to *E* magazine, it takes 2,500 gallons of water to produce one pound of meat, versus 25 gallons for a pound of wheat. It takes 16 pounds of grain to produce a single pound of beef, but only one pound of grain to produce a pound of bread. Meat production also uses more energy than growing vegetables and grains. By one estimate, a 10% reduction in beef consumption in the United States would free up enough land, water, and energy to feed 60 million people.

Red meat consumption declined by 39% during the 1980s, spurred on by health considerations including fat and cholesterol levels and contamination from antibiotics and hormones. The health and environmental impacts of cattle raising suggest opportunities for emerging technologies that can yield leaner beef with less environmental impact; however, given burgeoning population growth, a long-term shift from red meat to protein sources that are lower on the food chain seems inevitable.

Riding both health and environmental trends, vegetarianism, now being practiced by only 3% of the population in the United States, shows signs of becoming mainstream over the long term. In late 1991, *The Wall Street Journal* proclaimed that "vegetarianism is in at the nation's restaurants," and Eric Miller, writing in the *Research Alert* consumer trends letter noted in its October 18, 1991 issue: "The all-American burger is under siege. Pizza is gaining as the number one choice when eating out—now a mere four percentage points behind—with burgers slipping fast. Since 1987, burger orders dropped 7%, while pizza rose 12%." Indeed, McDonald's McLean burger is made with seaweed gums, and college campuses have installed vegetarian dining rooms, and celebrities like Linda McCartney may help to make vegetarianism chic. A line of vegetarian entries using McCartney as spokeswoman has been introduced into the United Kingdom and investors are being sought in the United States.[13]

Organic farming methods including composting, crop rotation, and integrated pest management help to prevent top soil erosion that occurs in the United States alone at the rate of three billion tons per year. While still not mainstream, the sales of organic foods has been strong over the past decade. The market now accounts for an estimated $1.4 billion in annual sales and is growing at the rate of 5–30% per year in some sectors. Low consumer demand for organics may trace back to an average 15% price premium that is not offset by a clear understanding of the health or environmental benefits of organic foods, but market dynamics promise to change that soon. As a result of the 1990 Farm Bill, federal standards for certified organically grown foods will go into effect in 1993 allowing manufacturers to make claims that will be meaningful to consumers. Thanks to improved trucking and warehousing methods, quality has improved dramatically in the past five years, and the market is responding. Major chains such as Vons and Lucky's are starting to carry organic foods. Companies such as Welch's and Smuckers are acquiring organic food producers.

SOLID WASTE MANAGEMENT

As depicted in Exhibit E.2, by 2010, Americans are expected to generate a total of 250.6 million tons of garbage per year, representing a 40% increase over 1988. This increase reflects two factors: a growing population and additional consumption of less durable products. In particular, the tonnage of plastics and paper is projected to grow at a great rate, while the other components of the waste stream, such as glass, metal, food, and yard waste, are projected to remain stable. (See Exhibit E.2.) With the number of landfills dropping precipitously from 18,000 in 1979 to an estimated 1,500 in 2003, there are many opportunities for manufacturers who can design products and packaging that utilize fewer resources, use recycled content, or otherwise help cut down on waste.

Now being explored for laundry products (see Chapter 5), refills and concentrates may be appropriate for other categories as well. For example, an entrepreneur and dentist in Houston has obtained a patent on a way to prepare mouthwash and medicine in powder form. The powder dissolves in water, or "fizzes into action," when placed in the mouth. The powdered preparations are considered to be more convenient than liquids because they can be carried compactly. Outside of their environmental benefits of cutting down on packaging, they also provide a health benefit. The formulations allow alcohol to be replaced with surfactants such as those used in toothpastes.[14]

As the market for refills and concentrates develops, opportunities will be created for permanent packages—spray bottles and detergent jugs offered to complement their use. Like their counterparts in Germany who bring back empty milk bottles for refilling in stores, some U.S. con-

EXHIBIT E.2
U.S. Municipal Solid Waste Generation

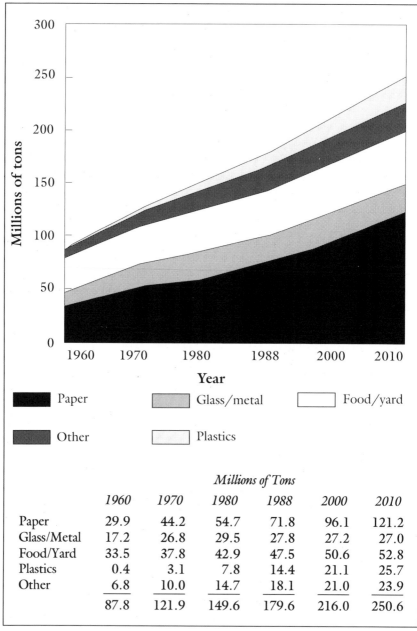

	1960	*1970*	*1980*	*1988*	*2000*	*2010*
Paper	29.9	44.2	54.7	71.8	96.1	121.2
Glass/Metal	17.2	26.8	29.5	27.8	27.2	27.0
Food/Yard	33.5	37.8	42.9	47.5	50.6	52.8
Plastics	0.4	3.1	7.8	14.4	21.1	25.7
Other	6.8	10.0	14.7	18.1	21.0	23.9
	87.8	121.9	149.6	179.6	216.0	250.6

Source: U.S. EPA, "Characterization of Municipal Solid Waste in the United States: 1990 Update," Executive Summary, Figure ES-6.

sumers already bring water bottles back to stores to refill from special vending machines. As the Body Shop's experience suggests, opportunities may exist to extend this practice to other types of liquids such as liquid detergents, milk, or even mouthwash and shampoo.

While aluminum cans, glass bottles, and plastic bottles used for soft drinks are recycled at impressive levels, technology also exists to eliminate the need for much of the bottle and can processing and energy involved in the transportation of these products. The Drinkmakr Company now markets a carbonation unit that allows consumers to make popular brands of soda pop at home using syrup purchased from local bottlers. The device helps consumers save money while reducing the need to transport 180 cans per month in high soft drink consuming households.[15] Coca-Cola is now marketing a similar device to small businesses.

Biodegradability may become a technically feasible solid waste solution for many types of plastics. According to *Green Marketing Report*, a food scientist at Oregon State University has come up with what may be the ultimate in green packaging: edible packaging made from corn protein, cellulose, and casings of shellfish. The tasteless and colorless film has been approved by the federal government for food packaging, and several food companies are reportedly interested. Similarly, the Novon Plastics Division of the Warner-Lambert Company is developing grades of specialty polymers derived from corn and potato starch that yield plastics that will safely decompose in a marine environment. Novon's goal is to develop cups, food wraps, eating utensils, diaper films, and tampon applicators that will safely degrade when composted on land or dumped at sea.[16]

Just a few years ago products made from recycled content were the exception, but one day soon they may represent the rule. While more and more recyclables are being collected, the market for products made from recycled content has barely been tapped. Some companies have been reluctant to manufacture recycled paper and plastics until they are assured that the supply of collected materials will remain steady and the demand will remain high. Also, recycled paper and plastics now sell for a higher price than virgin alternatives because of government subsidies on virgin timber and petroleum. This has created a glut of recyclable materials in many markets and caused prices to plunge. However, this may change. Laws, executive orders, and programs favoring recycled products are on the books in all 50 U.S. states, and the EPA has mandated federal government procurement guidelines for the $190 billion budget for food and services. Uniform guidelines for environmental marketing claims may be promulgated in the next few years through the legislative process and the EPA. These initiatives will encourage the development of economically efficient markets for products manufactured with recycled materials.

Currently, manufacturers are struggling (and paying the price) to make many types of products made from recycled materials look like virgin-quality material, but this may change as consumers increasingly accept differences that exist in products made with recycled as opposed to virgin materials. Indeed, flannel-look paper signifying recycled content is a plus to many consumers and to businesses desirous of projecting an environmentally responsible image. Acceptance of the unbleached, brown coffee filters and shipping cartons such as those now being used by Apple suggest that consumers may be increasingly willing to accept that purity and safety need no longer be translated to whiteness. In Europe, this new aesthetic is already being extended to many other types of paper products such as paper toweling, baby diapers, and feminine protection.

Opportunities for selling used products and for leasing durable products and major appliances may only have scratched the surface. Product obsolescence, once in vogue, may from a sociological and ecological standpoint become obsolete itself. In the future, consumers may favor old rather than new products as they merge their desires for quality, affordability, and environmental preservation. As Allan Magrath pointed out in *Marketing News,* more and more consumers now seek products with enduring value and high-quality craftsmanship such as antiques, century-old homes, and bathtubs with claw feet. Consumers have long appreciated the economic benefits of buying products such as used cars, furniture, appliances, clothing, textbooks, and, increasingly, computers. Economic forces currently favor a growing market for used items—of course these often sell at a favorable discount.[17] In the automobile industry two million "almost-new" cars (representing 25% of new car sales) were sold to consumers in 1991. New car dealers who resell these cars purchased from rental companies report that they make more money selling an almost-new car than they do selling a brand new one.[18]

A strategy long used for cars and furniture, leasing may emerge as a profitable strategy for major appliances such as refrigerators that can be re-manufactured or upgraded and leased to consumers several times.

PROTECTION FROM ENVIRONMENTAL ILLS

A final area of opportunity lies in helping consumers to protect themselves from the health risks represented by environmental ills such as ozone layer depletion and indoor air pollution. Indeed, marketers are already developing a number of opportunities:

• A Chicago-based company, Solar Protection Factory, Inc., has introduced a nylon-based cloth—Solarweave—that blocks 90% of the sun's UV-B rays and 93% of UV-A rays. Most cloth used for T-shirts block 50% of all UV rays.[19]

• According to *Advertising Age*, sales of sunless tanning products grew 50% in 1991 on the strength of consumers' desire to achieve the glow of a healthy tan without the cancer concerns associated with direct sunbathing.[20]

• Sun aversion is already becoming an operative in many consumer product categories like cosmetics and moisturizers. As the ozone layer further depletes, sunscreens may become obligatory in all skin and eyecare products, and sunblocking technology may become mandatory in windows and in car windshields.

• Environmentally sensitive home construction is now a booming business. Eco-buildings and healthy houses incorporate advanced energy designs and use materials that are non-toxic and recyclable. As reported by *The New York Times*, healthy homes, developed initially for the highly allergic consumer, are increasingly being requested by the growing legion of consumers with environmental and chemical sensitivities. These homes use non-toxic products such as natural floor finishes and non-petroleum based paints and insulation made from seawater and cement. Such alternatives cut down on adverse health effects ranging from headaches, insomnia, and skin rashes to severe joint pain, anxiety, and depression.[21]

- 3M has introduced the Filtrete Clean Air Filter, which traps 92% of airborne dust, pollen, and mold, and cleans air 20 times more effectively than traditional filters used in furnaces and home air conditioners. Through these filters, 3M has responded to heightened consumer awareness of indoor air quality issues and the resulting demand for a more benign indoor environment. The filters especially appeal to allergy sufferers. JoAnn Fernandez, marketing operations manager for 3M's Do-It-Yourself division, notes, "We have seen increased consumer and government awareness of indoor air quality issues, while noting the absence of product innovation to improve the performance of filters used in homes."

How to Get a Jump on the Future

- Set up a long-term monitoring system to keep abreast of pertinent developments. Track consumer attitudes, emerging environmental ills, and legislative and regulatory trends through proprietary research studies, environmental group communiques, government publications, and issue-specific newsletters. Develop alliances with some of the constituencies that are driving green issues such as special interest groups, scientists, economists, and government leaders.

- Find out how green your future is by asking questions such as:

  1. What technological developments could influence our products and packaging?
  2. What legislative or regulatory initiatives are likely to affect our business?
  3. What developments in Europe and Japan may impact the U.S. market and/or directly affect our business?
  4. What shifts in consumer attitudes are expected in the next 5–10 years?
  5. What are the implications for our business of environmental issues such as solid waste, global climate changes, carbon dioxide emissions, indoor air pollution, ozone layer depletion, chemophobia?

• Develop new product opportunities aimed at helping to solve problems relating to environment—the land, the water, the air. Seek out opportunities to solve regional issues.

A Final Word

By now it should be clear that environmental consumerism is not a fad or even a short-term trend. It is a way of life with broad support throughout our society. A new marketing age is upon us, requiring a sincere commitment to reconciling the needs of the environment with those of the consumer. Marketers who do this successfully will reap an abundance of rewards: added market share, enhanced imagery, increased profits, not to mention the personal rewards of doing business within the confines of the highest possible environmental and social ethics.

The strategies depicted in this book are general in nature: truly successful marketers will carve out their own distinctive approaches for addressing consumers' environmental concerns based on factors such as their industry, corporate heritage, and brand image. Like many of the marketers described in this book, they will pioneer strategies that uniquely leverage corporate and brand strengths while sending a clear message to consumers that their company genuinely cares and that consumers can make a difference by buying their products.

Imagination, creativity, and the ability to think in new ways will be critical to developing the many opportunities of environmental consumerism. The most daring marketers—and those with potentially the most to gain—may even reinvent their companies and their products in the quest for solutions that can lead to long-term competitive advantage.

Notes

1. Speth, James Gustave, "The Environment Agenda for Leaders," *Directors & Boards,* Summer 1991, p.5–6.

2. Brown, Lester R., *et al., Saving the Planet: How to Shape an Environmentally Sustainable Economy,* W. W. Norton & Company, 1991, p.118.

3. Link Resources Group, as reported in *Green MarketAlert,* July 1991.

4. "Bellying Up to the Bar Code," *Time,* Jan. 20, 1992, p. 38.

5. *Green MarketAlert,* July 1991.

6. Lowe, Marcia A., "The Bicycle: Vehicles for a Small Planet," Worldwatch Institute, p.90.

7. Dolan, Carrie, "Californians Already Laid Back Will Now Be Free Wheeling, Too," *The Wall Street Journal,* Feb. 21, 1992.

8. *Is It Really Green?* Seventh Generation, Colchester, VT, 1990.

9. Brown, Lester R., *et al., Saving the Planet: How to Shape an Environmentally Sustainable Economy,* W. W. Norton & Company, 1991, p.117.

10. Kahn, Alfred E., "Environmentalists Hijack the Utility Regulations," *The Wall Street Journal,* Aug. 7, 1991.

11. Smith, Emily, *et al.,* "Growth vs. Environment," *Business Week,* May 11, 1992, p.70.

12. Brenny, Jan, "Make Room for Water Savers," *Hardware Age,* Apr. 1992, p.66.

13. Dagnoli, Judann, and Wentz, Laurel, "Are You Ready for Food by Linda McCartney?" *Advertising Age,* Mar. 1992, p.1.

14. "A Powdered Mouthwash with Fizz," *The New York Times,* Jan .24, 1990.

15. Ottman, Jacquelyn A., "New Year's Resolution: Take a Great Leap Forward," *Green Marketing Report,* Jan. 1991, p.9.

16. *Business and the Environment,* Mar. 1992, p.13.

17. Magrath, Allan J., "If Used Product Sellers Ever Get Organized, Watch Out," *Marketing News,* June 25, 1990, p.8.

18. Levin, Doron P., "Almost New Is Good Enough, Much to Detroit's Annoyance," *The New York Times,* May 28, 1991, p.1.

19. *EcoSource,* Vol.2, No.3, 1991, p.17.

20. Sloan, Pat, "Sunless Tans Shine," *Advertising Age,* Mar. 16, 1992, p.16.

21. Ravo, Nick, "Environmentally Sensitive Construction," *The New York Times,* Jan. 12, 1992, p.6.

For Further Information

Abt Associates, Inc.
55 Wheeler Street
Cambridge, MA 02138
617/492-7100

Arthur D. Little Company
25 Acorn Park
Cambridge, MA 02140
617/864-5770

Cambridge Reports Trends &
    Forecasts
675 Massachusetts Avenue,
    4th Floor
Cambridge, MA 02139
617/661-0110

Council on Economic Priorities
30 Irving Place
New York, NY 10003
212/420-1133

DDB Needham Worldwide
437 Madison Avenue
New York, NY 10022
212/415-2000

Environmental Defense Fund
257 Park Avenue South
New York, NY 10010
212/505-2100

Federal Trade Commission
6th Street & Pennsylvania Avenue,
    NW
Washington, DC 20580
202/326-2000

Find/SVP
625 Avenue of the Americas
New York, NY 10011
212/645-4500

Friends of the Earth
530 7th Street, SE
Washington, DC 20003
202/544-2600

The Gallup Organization
100 Palmer Square, Suite 200
Princeton, NJ 08542
609/924-9600

Gerstman & Meyers
111 West 57th Street
New York, NY 10019
212/307-5473

Good Housekeeping Institute
Bureau of Chemistry and
    Environmental Science
959 Eighth Avenue
New York, NY 10019
212/649-2000

Green Seal Incorporated
1250 23rd Street, NW
Washington, DC 20037
202/331-7337

Hubert H. Humphrey III
State Attorney General
102 State Capitol
St. Paul, MN 55155
612/296-6196

Institute of Packaging Professionals
481 Carlisle Drive
Herndon, VA 22070
703/318-8970

Keep America Beautiful
9 West Broad Street
Stamford, CT 06902
203/323-8987

Marketing Intelligence Service Ltd.
33 Academy Street
Naples, NY 14512
716/374-6326

National Audubon Society
950 Third Avenue
New York, NY 10022
212/832-3200

National Wildlife Federation
1400 Sixteenth Street, NW
Washington, DC 20036-2266
202/797-6800

Nature Conservancy
1815 Lynn Street
Arlington, VA 22209
703/379-8761

Natural Resources Defense Council
40 West 20th Street
New York, NY 10010
212/727-2700

J. Ottman Consulting
1133 Broadway
Suite 1211
New York, NY 10010
212/255-3800

Pennsylvania Resources Council
Box 88
Media, PA 19063
215/565-9131

Rocky Mountain Institute
1739 Snowmass Creek Road
Snowmass, CO 81654-9199
303/927-3851

The Roper Organization
205 East 42nd Street
New York, NY 10017
212/599-0700

Scientific Certification Systems
1611 Telegraph Avenue
Suite 1111
Oakland, CA 94612
510/832-1415

Sierra Club
730 Polk Street
San Francisco, CA 94109
415/776-2211

Solid Waste Composting Council
114 South Pitt Street
Alexandria, VA 22314
800/285-6064

United States Environmental
  Protection Agency
401 "M" Street, NW
Washington, DC 20460
202/382-2090

United States Public Interest
  Groups, Inc.
215 Pennsylvania Avenue, SE
Washington, DC 20003
202/546-9707

Warwick Baker & Fiore
100 Avenue of Americas
New York, NY 10013
212/941-4200

Washington Citizens for Recycling
216 First Avenue South, #360
Seattle, WA 98104
206/343-5171

World Resources Institute
1709 New York Avenue, NW
  7th Fl.
Washington, DC 20006
202/638-6300

World Wildlife Fund
1250 24th Street, NW
Washington, DC 20037
202/293-4800

Worldwatch Institute
1776 Massachusetts Avenue
Washington, DC 20036
202/452-1999

Yankelovich Clancy Shulman
8 Wright Street
Westport, CT 06877
203/227-2700

For Further Reading

Business Resources

Assessing the Environmental Consumer Market: 40 Case Studies, U.S. Environmental Protection Agency, Office of Policy, Planning and Evaluation, Washington, D.C., 1991.

Beyond Compliance, Bruce Smart, ed., World Resources Institute, Washington, D. C.

Business Ethics Magazine, Marjorie Kelly, ed., Mavis Publications, Chaska, MN.

Changing Corporate Values, Richard Adams, *et al.*, Kogan Page Ltd., London, England. A guide to social and environmental policy and practice in Britain's top companies.

Design for the Environment, Dorothy Mackenzie, Rizzoli International Publications, New York, NY.

Design for Recycling: A Plastic Bottle Recycler's Perspective, Richard A. Fleming, Partnership for Plastics Progress, The Society of the Plastics Industry, Washington, D.C.

DMA Environmental Resource for Direct Marketers, Direct Marketing Association, New York, NY, 1990.

Green Company Resource Guide: Leading Resources for Environmentally Sound Business, The New Consumer Institute, Wauconda, IL.

Green is Gold, Patrick Carson and Julia Moulden, Harper Business, Toronto, Ontario, 1991.

Green MarketAlert, monthly newsletter, MarketAlert Publications, Bethlehem, CT.

Green Marketing Report, bi-monthy newsletter, Business Publishers, Inc., Silver Spring, MD.

Green 2000, monthly packaging newsletter, Packaging Strategies, West Chester, PA.

173

In Business, magazine for environmental entrepreneurs, Jerome Goldstein, ed., The JG Press, Inc., Emmaus, PA.

State Recycling Laws Update, Raymond Communications, Riverdale, MD, 1992.

Consumer Resources

Buzzworm: The Environmental Journal, Joseph E. Daniel, ed., Buzzworm, Inc., Boulder, CO.

E. The Environmental Magazine, Doug Moss, ed., Earth Action Network, Norwalk, CT.

Garbage, Patricia Poore, ed., Old House Journal Corp., Brooklyn, NY.

Sierra, Jonathan F. King, ed., Sierra Club, San Francisco.

50 Simple Things You Can Do to Save the Earth, The EarthWorks Group, Earthworks Press, Berkeley, CA.

The Green Consumer, John Elkington, Julia Hailes, and Joel Makower, Penguin Press, New York, 1990.

Plagued by Packaging: A Consumer Guide to Excess Packaging and Disposable Waste Problems, The NY Public Interest Research Group, New York, NY.

Shopping for a Better World: A Quick and Easy Guide to Socially Responsible Supermarket Shopping, Ben Corson, *et al.*, Council on Economic Priorities, New York, NY, 1992.

General

Conservation Directory of Environmental Organizations, National Wildlife Federation, Washington, D.C.

Environmental Almanac, World Resources Institute, Houghton Mifflin Company, Boston, MA, 1992.

State of the World, Lester Brown, *et al.*, World Watch, W. W. Norton & Company, New York, NY, 1992.

INDEX

177